Buddhism
and the Claims
of Christ

Buddhism and the Claims of Christ

BY D.T. NILES

1368

JOHN KNOX PRESS
Richmond, Virginia

To
the memory of
Hendrik Kraemer
and
Paul Devanandan

Contents

Preface

BUDDHISM AND THE CLAIMS OF CHRIST was first published in Ceylon in 1946. Two decades later, the opportunity has come to have it published also in the West. In getting it ready for publication, I have not attempted to change its style or method of presentation. These were originally determined by the reasons that prompted me to write it: to state the Christian faith in Buddhist idiom, to make use of the "form" in which Buddhist teaching is usually presented, to put into small compass the essentials of the Christian faith so that it can serve as a book of instruction for catechumens whose background was Buddhism. The large number of references to Christian Scripture is deliberate. A catechumen will need to be introduced to the Christian Scriptures. The same reason prompted the use I have made of the Apostles' Creed and the Lord's Prayer.

Recently the Reverend Gerald H. Anderson edited a book entitled *Sermons to Men of Other Faiths and Traditions,* published by Abingdon Press. I was asked to send a contribution for this symposium. I sent, as a sermon addressed to Buddhists, the first chapter of this book. At that time, I had no notion that the book as a whole would get a chance to be re-published. The permission for the chapter to remain part of this book is here gladly acknowledged, both to Rev. Gerald Anderson and to his publisher.

When the book was published in Ceylon, it bore a foreword from Bishop Lakdasa de Mel, now Metropolitan of the Church of India, Pakistan, Burma, and Ceylon. The book owes not a little to the wise encouragement I received from him. This is what he wrote:

> It is with great pleasure that I commend this timely book which attempts to set forth the writer's deepest convictions in a spirit that leaves old methods and controversies behind. Here is an explanation of the fundamental Christian beliefs written not only in a friendly and understanding spirit but also in the idiom familiar to our Buddhist friends. Further there is an objectiveness that is refreshing, the writer bringing an acute mind from North Ceylon to bear on discussions which have so far been practically monopolised by the South.
>
> Though this book is addressed to Buddhists, Christians also will find its presentation of the Christian faith in fresh thought forms both profitable and illuminating. Besides, the author's extensive use of Christian scripture should help both the Christian and the Buddhist reader. It should serve to show that here is no attempt at syncretism but that what is presented is indeed the Christian faith. The Buddhist, no less than the Christian, must find it rewarding to follow out the scripture references in their contexts.
>
> I congratulate the author and wish this book much usefulness.

When Hendrik Kraemer saw this book, he asked me to get it published in the West also and kindly sent me, at my request, a foreword to be used when this happened. It is this foreword that I have now used.

Hendrik Kraemer and Paul Devanandan are the two men to whom I am most indebted for the way in which I have learned to study other religions and to be in normal converse with adherents of these religions. Kraemer taught me to approach other faiths and to enter into them as a Christian; Devanandan taught me to see and understand the Christian faith from the vantage ground of other faiths.

To the memory of both these men this little book is dedicated in admiration, gratitude, and affection.

D. T. Niles

Foreword

In 1938, during the World Missionary Conference at Tambaram, one of the central subjects was "the Christian Message in a non-Christian world," and the underlying problem how to state the relation of the content of the biblical revelation to the whole field of historical and other religions. The controversy at last moved around the terms: Continuity or Discontinuity. One might say also: Fulfillment or Judgment.

Now Rev. D. T. Niles, who as a student of religion and as an evangelist has been occupied by this fundamental problem, especially in regard to Buddhism, has had the excellent idea of stating the conclusions of his thinking not in the abstract, but in a concrete presentation of the Christian message in vital confrontation and contact with the essential tenets of Buddhism. In his presentation he has tried to preach Christ as the power and the wisdom of God, by becoming a Buddhist to the Buddhists. He has consistently striven toward using the cardinal concepts and terms of Buddhism to convey the Christian message and its essential character.

It seems to me that Dr. Niles has done his job very ably, and in a way that commands serious attention. By this concrete, vivid method of treating a fundamental theological and religious problem he has succeeded in striking a right balance in the confrontation of Buddhism and Christianity. Just because his Christian sensitiveness is open to the fertilizing influence of Buddhism on his faith and understanding, he is able to demonstrate that Buddhism in no sense affords a foundation on which the Christian faith can be based. In Christ all things really become new.

This small book is therefore a real contribution to our theological and missionary thinking. I commend it heartily to the world of theologians and missionaries.

H. Kraemer

Introduction*

CHRISTIAN. What are you doing this evening, anything special?

1ST BUDDHIST. No, nothing. Why?

CHRISTIAN. I was wondering whether you would care to go with me to a meeting to be held at the Y.M.C.A. The address is to be on "Eternal Life—Now."

1ST BUDDHIST. But what does that mean?

CHRISTIAN. I think that the lecture is to be an exposition of the meaning of the Christian faith and its relevance for today.

1ST BUDDHIST. Is the speaker good?

CHRISTIAN. He is not much of an orator, but there is content in his message.

1ST BUDDHIST. I am afraid I can't come. Honestly, I have come to doubt the relevance of all religions.

CHRISTIAN. What do you mean?

1ST BUDDHIST. I mean this, that all religions are played out. They are all forms of escape from the tragedy of living. Think of that lecture on the *dhamma,* for instance, which was delivered at the college.

2ND BUDDHIST (*passing that way joins in*). What about that lecture on the *dhamma?*

1ST BUDDHIST. The lecturer said that we must pass beyond moral striving to a realization of *nibbana,* remembering that life

---

* In this book the spelling of Buddhist terms differs slightly from that most familiar to Westerners; for instance, *nibbana,* not *nirvana,* and *kamma,* not *karma.* This is done in order to follow consistently the spelling in Pali, the original language of the Buddhist scriptures.

13

as we live it is unreal since it is ignorantly lived. He stressed the fact that we had no self-identity, and that, therefore, there was no meaning in any achievement of the self. I ask you, does not the whole thing look like a way of escape from the realities of life's responsibility and the obligations of morality?

2ND BUDDHIST. But then, did not the lecturer say that moral living was a necessary discipline, a necessary preliminary on the way to that complete denial of the self to attain which is *nibbana?*

1ST BUDDHIST. Yes, but if one has to achieve moral living as a preliminary to attaining *nibbana,* one may as well not begin. It is the moral problem that constitutes life's tragedy, and what is the use of telling us to solve it so that we may be able to attain something else? I don't want to solve or attain anything else.

CHRISTIAN. What do you mean by the moral problem?

1ST BUDDHIST. I mean the injustices of life, the glibness with which some, like the communists and the war-mongers, advocate further acts of injustice as a means of achieving justice, and one's own inability to do anything. Besides, there is the feeling of moral bankruptcy in the depths of one's nature caused by an inescapable idealism which is, however, impossible of achievement.

2ND BUDDHIST. I believe that Buddhism offers a way out of this despair which you are describing. It teaches us that *nibbana* is attained at the end of a long process, stage by stage, bit by bit, through life after life. Despair is simply the result of impatience.

1ST BUDDHIST. That is another way of escape. It is useless to say that the availability of infinite time makes a problem solvable, when it is the nature of the problem that defies solution. The moral problem is not that there is not sufficient time in which I and society can become good, but that I and society cannot become good.

CHRISTIAN. Let me ask you a question about something you said earlier. You said that communists and war-mongers advocated unjust ways of achieving justice. Are you fair in such a statement?

1ST BUDDHIST. Why not? Don't the communists want to get rid of the capitalists, even by shooting them if necessary? They argue that you can be unjust to one generation in order to achieve justice for the next: but don't you see that if you can be unjust to one generation, then you can be unjust to another also? As for war-mongers, don't they talk of the relative justice of a cause, as if when you serve a cause which is relatively just, you thereby serve the demand of your nature for goodness?

2ND BUDDHIST. But don't you? Goodness demands that I do the lesser evil.

1ST BUDDHIST. No, goodness demands that I do no evil; and when circumstances force me to choose the lesser *evil* because I must be *good,* then it is that I am in the grip of moral tragedy.

2ND BUDDHIST. Now I begin to see a little why Buddhist people have grafted into their religion the element of devotion to God, often to the Buddha himself conceived of as God. In any case, there is no mistaking the worship aspect of Buddhism today.

CHRISTIAN. I wonder what you mean.

2ND BUDDHIST. Don't you see that since the purely ethical formulation of religion leads to a sense of frustration, people have found release through worship: for worship means that the ultimate demand on me is not the demand of goodness but of devotion.

1ST BUDDHIST. I have never been able to understand why anyone should go into ecstasies about God.

2ND BUDDHIST. Because he is God—don't you see that that is what God is for!

CHRISTIAN. We love God because he first loved us.

2ND BUDDHIST. Now you are going to talk the usual drivel about Jesus dying for us poor men.

CHRISTIAN. Not if you don't want me to. Look at it this way, however . . .

1ST BUDDHIST. Wait a minute—even if there is a God, what has Jesus got to do with him? Why must I love God, as you say, because of what Jesus did?

CHRISTIAN. We do not love God because of Jesus. We love Jesus, and find that in loving him we love God. The first question, however, is, "Is Jesus lovable? Has he solved the problem of goodness?"

1ST BUDDHIST. I would say Yes and No. He was good. But

that only makes the problem worse. In fact I have often felt, in discussing these things with Christians and in reading some of their books, that it was because Jesus makes the problem of goodness worse that Christianity has changed the Way of Jesus too into a way of escape from the problem of living.

CHRISTIAN. What do you mean?

1ST BUDDHIST. How many Christians accept the life of Jesus as an example that *can* be followed, not *ought* to be followed; and how many Christians accept the teachings of Jesus as meant for direct and literal application to the problems of today?

2ND BUDDHIST. You are right. I have sometimes gone to the S.C.M. discussion group at College, and nothing has struck me there more than the attempts that are made to justify the Christians, the Christian church, and the so-called Christian nations by watering down the teachings of Jesus.

CHRISTIAN. I'll accept the condemnation of institutional Christianity and of Christians implied in what you say, but are you fair to Jesus when you say that he makes the problem of goodness worse? Judged by the obvious and insistent problems of his day, the life of Jesus was largely an irrelevance. He had no program for the achievement of Jewish independence. He conducted no campaign for the enactment of juster laws. He put forward no plans for the reconstruction of village or town life. He advocated no solution . . .

2ND BUDDHIST. Are you then saying that Jesus does not make the problem of goodness worse because his life is an irrelevance?

CHRISTIAN. No, what I am saying is that the relevance of the life of Jesus for all time lies in its irrelevance to his own times. The solution of Jesus to the problem of goodness lies in his achievement of goodness through a life of irrelevance.

1ST BUDDHIST. I don't follow you.

CHRISTIAN. Isn't the tragedy of living accentuated for us because we try to live a life that is too total an attempt to meet life's immediate problems? We live too completely in one dimension, the dimension of our own time. Jesus has shown us that there is a second dimension, the dimension of God's eternal purpose.

1ST BUDDHIST. But is that not an attempt to escape from present issues?

CHRISTIAN. Yes, but we must escape from present issues to the extent that these issues are not the strategic expression in the present of the eternal conflict between God and evil, but are, as it were, side-issues.

2ND BUDDHIST. I am surprised that so far you have not referred to the death of Jesus.

CHRISTIAN. You wished me not to, but now that you ask about it, I suppose you can see its relationship to what we have been talking about.

1ST BUDDHIST. I don't. Jesus died a martyr.

CHRISTIAN. No, Jesus died having been made "sin." For him too, since he was man, there was no escape from the problem of goodness. But he chose to live so completely in terms of God's eternal will that his life became a complete refusal to live only in his present. This refusal he made unto death. When I say, therefore, that Jesus died for me, I mean that because of his death I am delivered from seeking the good life, the life of obedience to a moral ideal, a life of despair which accumulates condemnation unto death; and I am committed to live a life of devotion to Jesus, the end of which is complete freedom.

1ST BUDDHIST. I am not sure that I understand everything of what you have been saying—for that matter I wonder whether you have a clear idea yourself—but . . .

CHRISTIAN. You are quite right. As I think of the death of Jesus in relation to his life and my life and the life of the world, I feel something which I cannot quite express. Perhaps the simplest way of showing you the direction of my thinking is to say that when I look at the Cross I have no more desire to make goodness as such my life's aim.

1ST BUDDHIST. It strikes me that this at least is true, that the relevance of Jesus to my life and yours is the relevance of Eternity to time. Buddhism ultimately sets time and Eternity in opposition, and bids us somehow deny time on behalf of Eternity; while, if I understand aright, Jesus bids us live in time as if we were living in Eternity.

CHRISTIAN. Yes, I think that that expresses it. Now what about going to the meeting this evening?

1ST BUDDHIST *(to the 2nd Buddhist)*. Will you come too? There is to be an address at the Y.M.C.A. this evening on "Eternal Life—Now."

2ND BUDDHIST. Yes.

PART I:
TOWARD UNDERSTANDING

Do not go merely by hearsay or
tradition, not by what has been handed
down from olden time, not by rumours,
not by mere reasoning and logical
deductions, not by outward appear-
ances, not by cherished opinions and
speculations, not by mere possibil-
ities, and do not believe merely
because I am your master. But when
you yourselves have seen that a thing
is evil and leads to harm and suffering
then you should reject it. And when
you see that a thing is good and blame-
less, and leads to blessing and welfare,
then you should do such a thing.*

Gotama Buddha

---

* *Kalama Sutta.*

1.

The Christian Perspective

Dear Friend,

You have taken up this book to read it, because you are interested in the Christian faith and way of life and would like to understand them. I have written this book because I have been interested in the Buddhist *dhamma* and way of life and have sought to understand them, and would now seek to share what I have learned as Buddhist faith and Christian faith illumined one another in my own life and understanding.

The Buddha has said that no one should be bound by any authority, not even that of the Buddha, but that each should accept and follow that which commends itself to reason and conscience. Here is your standing ground as a Buddhist in seeking to understand someone of another faith. What is my standing ground as a Christian? I can state it best by referring to a passage in a letter of Paul, the Apostle, written to his friend Philemon in which he says, "I pray that the sharing of your faith may promote the knowledge of all the good that is ours in Christ" (Philem. 6). Paul, as you can see, is making here a double emphasis: All good is ours in Christ. The good that is in Christ is ours—yours and mine together.

A. THE TRUTH OF BUDDHISM

In the course of this book you will find that I use words and ideas with which you are familiar as a Buddhist; you will also find that these words and ideas are set in a context often different from and sometimes even contradictory to their natural context

21

in Buddhism. You may want to ask the question whether I have the right so to use these words and ideas, since every religion is a totality, and ideas in it derive their meaning from their place in that totality. Your question will be legitimate, but my answer is that I use these words and ideas not as intending to graft into the Christian faith elements of truth as I see them in Buddhism, but as attempting to state the Christian faith in language that already has significance for you. There is also a second answer on which this first answer is dependent, the answer that when I, as a Christian, came to study Buddhism I found that it fertilized my faith and enriched my understanding, so that these Buddhist terms and ideas have come to have a real meaning for me in the context of my own faith. Besides, this is what my faith too leads me to expect, for it asserts that *God has not left himself without witness among any people, and that it is in the purpose of this design to gather up all things in Christ in the fullness of time* (Acts 14:27; Eph. 1:10).

Religious truths do not meet in the library; they meet in the minds and souls of men, so that while to some extent a student can approach the study of a religion neutrally, he can never completely or even adequately do so. Thus I cannot formulate any general theory as to the relation between the Christian faith and the Buddhist *dhamma;* all that I can do is to present my faith as a Christian to you as a Buddhist in as meaningful a language for you as I am able to use, and then leave it at that. Perhaps I can do one other thing also, and that is to share with you frankly my own appraisal of Buddhism as a Christian student of it. Among the great religions of the world, Buddhism is one of the most realistic. It does not suffer from any cheap optimism either about man or about the world. Man is conceived of as man, without any attempt to rationalize or minimize his tragedy. Besides, the whole paraphernalia of practices by which men seek and have sought to invoke the intervention of the supernatural is markedly absent. The result of this whole attitude is that positively we have in Buddhism a diagnosis of life's problem which is radical in its insight; and, negatively, we are set free from all conceptions of God which treat him as a *deus ex machina*. It is right that a God whom men can manipulate should be jettisoned.

The peculiar faith of Christianity is that there are two points of view from which every truth must be approached—a human point of view and a divine. There is truth as man sees it from his predicament as man, and there is also truth as God reveals it to man in terms of God's own purpose for man and for the world: so that the whole truth lies in holding these both together under one insight. Thus, life judged from the human end alone leads men either to a dreaming about utopias or to a renunciation of life's responsibilities; while life judged from the divine end alone leads men either to a dreaming about millenniums or to a denial of the reality of our temporal existence. The whole truth is affirmed only when it is recognized that we may not speak about life without speaking simultaneously both about man and about God, and about man as man and God as God. Indeed, we state both sides of the truth only when we state them in tension—man in tension with God, and God in tension with man—for to fuse both together, as we do when we disguise man with divinity or enmesh God in human systems, is to destroy both.

What strikes a Christian student of Buddhism, therefore, is that he meets in Buddhism a description of life and the world from the human side without any attempt to camouflage the human situation: and also that he does not meet in Buddhism all those presuppositions about God as viewed from the human end which in other religions constitute such an obstacle to God's approach to man.

B. THE CLAIMS OF CHRIST

All this is not to say that I believe that you as a Buddhist will find it easy either to understand or to accept the truth of the Christian faith. You will not. For the whole point of Buddhism is the denial of the relevance, if not the existence, of this other side to life—the side which we have called divine. A study of Buddhism can fertilize the growth of understanding of the Christian faith; it can make for a formulation of Christian truth in Buddhist terms; but Buddhism as such affords no foundation on which the Christian faith can be based. In fact, when you face God as the Christian faith presents him, you do not face him as a Buddhist but as a man, and you will find what all other men have found—

whether they be Christians or Buddhists or Hindus or Muslims—
that when the self comes to its decisive meeting with God, the
chief hindrances to accepting him are the truths that it already
knows and the goodness which it already possesses. One of the
greatest Jews of his day found it to be so and expressed his
experience in these words: "But whatever gain I had, I counted
as loss for the sake of Christ. Indeed I count everything as loss
because of the surpassing worth of knowing Christ Jesus my
Lord" (Phil. 3:7-8).

I have said all this to you, because it is only fair by you and
myself and the nature of God's confrontation with man that I
should give you this warning. I dare not minimize the contradic-
tion that there is between faith in God and your natural presuppositions. God cannot be proved. To attempt to do so will be as
futile as to attempt to prove color to a blind man. All that one can
do is to show that the belief in God is reasonable, that it is on the
basis of such a belief that life is seen to be most meaningful,
and that there is ample witness for the truth of such a belief in
the living experience of men and women of every age and country and kind. Let me help you to say, "I wish it were true," and
then I know that you will see it to be true, because God himself
will give you sight.

Please do not misunderstand what I have said to imply that I
think that you as a Buddhist are peculiarly blind, and that unless
your blindness is cured you cannot appreciate truth in its wholeness. What I have tried to say rather is that you are blind exactly
in the same way in which we are all blind, until we realize our
blindness and ask that God give us sight. Whether we call ourselves Christians or Buddhists, we know and see this material life
and tend to deny any other reality, at least in practice. It is when
we become convinced of our own helplessness and the world's
hopelessness that we cry out for and receive both help and hope.

The Christian, when he receives his sight, begins to see the
truth of many of the things which his religion has been teaching
him all the time, and which he so far had tended to deny; the
Buddhist, when he receives his sight, begins to see that the many
things which he accepted as true are only partially so, and only
true in a new context and in relation to other truths.

P.8486

I wonder whether you think that I am presumptuous in saying this; perhaps I am—but the determining faith with which the Christian approaches any truth is the faith that Jesus Christ is the fullness of light. In Christ's presence everything is seen clearly and in its right proportions and relations. In the presence of light, only darkness melts away; everything else remains. In many cases the Christian context is revolutionary to the Buddhist concept, and yet the concept remains true; only, before this, its truth was misstated because it was stated from the human angle alone.

In saying this, I do not forget that for you the chief difficulty will be to accept that there is any other angle except the human; I should not be surprised if you thought sometimes that this belief in a Divine order of reality is simply a way of escape from the hardness of this life, a way of achieving compensation. My only answer is that those who have truly found and accepted God in Christ have also found that thereby they had been committed to a life such as Jesus himself lived, and, as you will agree, it is difficult to use the words "escape" and "compensation" about his life. Besides, if the truth be that there is a real escape from the tragedy of this life, real compensation and not fantasy, something that brings to this life true purposefulness and the courage to achieve while also giving assurance of a more abundant life after death, then it were folly to discredit it.

C. THE NATURE OF TRUTH

My attempt so far has been to explain to you the Christian perspective in general as a preparation for an ongoing discussion of the various dogmas of our faiths. But, as part of this preparation, another question too must be dealt with—that which concerns the nature of dogma itself.

Every religion has its own dogmas—the unproved and unprovable assumptions on which its whole outlook depends. You may demur and say that we must not assume anything without proof, but I would like to ask you what you do mean by proof after all. If by proof you mean that we must not believe in anything whose existence cannot be demonstrated in terms of the knowledge we already possess, then I should like to ask on what grounds the knowledge we already possess is assumed to be adequate so as to afford a criterion of proof. On this definition of proof we should not be able to believe either in God or in *nibbana*. If, on the other hand, by proof you mean that we should not believe in anything which cannot be made the subject of a demonstrable experiment in life, then I should gladly consent; only I could not agree that this would be proof at all, for such an experiment merely amounts to judging of the nature of something by its effects without getting to know the cause of these effects directly and integrally. It is on the basis of such experimental proof that you claim to believe in the doctrine of *kamma* and I in the doctrine of the atonement. This is just about all the proof that one can have about God too—a knowledge of him by his actions without any direct perception of him as he is.

If then we are committed in every religion to the acceptance of dogmas, how do we decide between them (for decide we must since the dogmas of the various religions are not mutually consistent)?

Thought always must have a starting point in an axiom; when we look at any religion we find that it takes its stand on a group of dogmas which are interdependent, and from that stand it seeks to explain life and its significance. When I say "explain," I mean that it seeks to relate the facts of life to its dogmas. And that is what "explanation" finally is. A thing is explained when its relationship to something else which is more directly known is demonstrated: so that a religious explanation of life means that beginning with certain dogmas the relationship between the various experiences and facts of life are set forth, the explanation returning ultimately to the dogmas.

True thought is always circular. It must lead up to its assumptions, and the difference between one circle of explanation and another circle is a difference of radius. Some explanations are so narrow that they leave much unexplained, especially much that is so important. The adequacy of truth in one religion as against another, therefore, is judged acccording as the circle of explanation of that religion includes the largest number of significant facts.

In an article in the Buddhist Annual of Ceylon of 1930, Buddhism is defined as "that religion which without starting with a God leads man to a stage where God's help is not necessary." That is true; it is also inevitable. If we do not start with God we shall not end with him, and when we start with him we do not end with the doctrines of *anicca, anatta,* and *dukkha.* The existence of God means the existence of an order of life which is eternal—*nicca.*[1] It means that there is postulated for the soul—*atta*—an identity which is guarded by God's sovereignty, and that sorrow—*dukkha*—is seen to consist, not so much in the transitoriness of things, as in the perverseness of our wills which seek these things instead of the things which are eternal. The circle of the Christian faith can thus be described as that which starting with God leads man to the realization that God alone affords the most adequate base for the most meaningful explanation of life's most significant facts.

You will notice that there is in this description of Christianity a use of the words "significant" and "meaningful" which is undefined. On what basis does one judge that this fact is more significant than that, or that this experience is more meaningful than another? Is there any basis at all for such judgment, or is not the truth rather this: that such judgments are purely relative and personal?

Here we come up against a further problem which must be clarified if we are to talk intelligently about truth at all: for if in our thinking about these large questions which involve the explanation of life's meaning, we necessarily think subjectively, then one man's answer is as true as another's, and there is no absolute standard of truth. A certain idea strikes one man as true because it "clicks" with the kind of man he is, and a contrary idea appeals to a man with a contrary character. We think with our character, and thought is not neutral. "The truth remains hidden from him whom desire and hate absorb" (*Vinaya Mahavagga*). True thought, therefore, depends on true character; or in other words, there can be no such thing as absolute goodness. Besides, it cannot be a thing either, for goodness is personal.

---

[1] *Anicca,* impermanence, is the opposite of *nicca,* permanence; *annata,* absence of self, is the opposite of *atta,* self.

We thus see the decisive significance for thought itself of the existence of God who is both truth and goodness and the standard for both: so that we are able to say that that thought is true which is in harmony with the thought of God. Once deny, however, that there is a God, and there is no escape from a utilitarian conception of goodness and a relativistic attitude to truth. This must not be misunderstood to mean that a good man can think correct mathematics. It means rather that where "truth" is concerned, truth not facts—truth is interpretative of life—goodness is its criterion.

This drama between the relative and the absolute was once played out in its final terms when Jesus stood before the Roman procurator—Pilate. To Pilate there was no such thing as truth; it was a question of what served. To Jesus, however, the determining fact was the truth which he served and which demanded from him the supreme sacrifice. "I have come . . . to bear witness to the truth," said Jesus; to which Pilate replied, "What is truth?" (John 18:37-38). What is truth indeed but God, and we think truly when we think God's thoughts after him.

Through long ages religion has been man's attempt to question the universe and wrest an answer from it as to its meaning. God was asked to justify himself before man, before man's needs, problems, desires, and standards; and as a result men have either shaped God in their own likeness—that is, to suit their prejudices—or they have denied God's relevance and even his existence. When you study the Christian faith, however, you will find that basically the position is reversed. It is man who has to justify himself before God's purposes and standards. The meaning of man's life is not in himself. Man is made for God, and men achieve their true destiny when they fulfill God's purpose for them.

Jesus, the Christian believes, is the revelation of God's purpose. In him, God confronts man and challenges him. True enough, Jesus has to win our allegiance, but in the final result we shall find that it is we who have to win his approval. He is the standard both of goodness and of truth. Truth cannot be a teaching; it has to be a person: for truth and goodness must cohere.

Jesus lived among men, and their witness was that they beheld his glory full of grace and truth (John 1:14).

D. IN QUEST OF MEANING

I have said that the adequacy of a truth depends on how large the circle is of significant facts which it explains; I must now go further and say that it is not you or I but God who should decide what facts are significant. In other words, those facts about which God has spoken are significant for life, and those facts about which he has not spoken are incidental. An example will make the meaning clear. There is not, for instance, in Christianity any explanation seeking to show that the experience of suffering is ordered by justice. On the other hand, the Christian faith, instead of seeking to invest the experience of suffering itself with meaning, deals with it as a fact to be used rather than to be justified. The determining motif is "Man's need of redemption and God's act to redeem him," and everything else, including the fact of suffering, is brought into relation with this motif. To anyone interested in the fact of suffering as such, this point of view of Christianity must necessarily seem disappointing, and yet for the person who has actually to deal with suffering, his own or another's, the Christian faith is full of meaning and of hope.

It is in an example such as this that one sees also most clearly the basic difference between Christianity and Buddhism, a difference that I must now try and state as plainly as possible. The difference it seems to me is this, that the Buddha saw that life was meaningless in itself and set out to rescue men from this meaninglessness.

Jesus, on the other hand, saw that life could become meaningful in God and set out to call men to share that meaning. "I came," he said, "that they may have life, and have it abundantly" (John 10:10). Your fundamental choice, therefore, is this: whether you would live life free from meaninglessness only or full of meaning. This is a fateful choice and an inevitable one.

Let me give an example of the difference it will make as to which path is chosen. History is moving on, and every race is struggling to live as meaningfully and as abundantly as possible.

This is the criterion by which a people's progress is judged. But do you agree that it should be so judged? And why should you agree, if life's primary task is to escape life's meaninglessness? A Christian, on the other hand, does speak of God as the God of history, as One whose purposes are being wrought on the historical plane. Thus, as a Christian, I am forced to take the life of my country and of my people seriously; I am bidden to do so by my faith, which also sets for me the perspective according to which I must think and act. Nationalism for me is a Christian duty; it is also bound by Christian standards. You too probably are a nationalist. Most of us do take the nation seriously these days. But what is the basis of nationalism in Buddhism? Race, nation, history—these are outside the Buddhist circle of explanation. To the Christian, however, they are significant facts and find inclusion in his faith.

I know that this difference in terms of meaning which I have pointed out between Buddhism and Christianity can be denied. For few Buddhists do in actual practice live as those who merely seek freedom from meaninglessness; they live, rather, as meaningfully as they can. Besides, the doctrine of the eightfold path itself lends support to this positive attitude. Yet the fact remains that the Buddha does treat death as life's appropriate adjective, while for Jesus it is not death but life which characterizes life.

Do I mean to say, then, that the life of the Buddha too was lived in terms of meaninglessness? No, for the Buddha dedicated his life to rescuing men from the despair and disillusion into which contemporary Hindu religion had led them. His was a protest against the cheap optimism engendered by the belief in the cosmic soul, against the fruitless salvation promised by the practices of formal religion, against the irresponsible freedom sought along the way of ascetic renunciation. The Buddha had a tremendous mission in his contemporary scene—hence the charm and strength of his life.

But no protest, however profound, can be turned into a religion; a religion demands primarily something to profess and live by rather than something to protest about and live against. For when the self has done protesting, it inevitably comes to its rude awakening under the challenge of life for responsible living. We can side-step that challenge for a time, but it has to be met, and be met more than empirically. Adequate religion means that it shows us the deepest level on which to meet life's challenge— the level of reality, of life's inner structure, of life's true base. It is in the exposition of this level that the fundamental differences of the various religions lie, and it is about this that they have their different dogmas.

To a discussion of these dogmas, both in Buddhism and Christianity, we must now turn.

2.

The Christian Dogmas

We have already discussed what a dogma is, so that you will understand when you find that in stating the Christian dogmas I have taken pains to show that these are not self-evident truths. Rather, they are truths which are asserted in the face of obvious contradictions, but asserted nevertheless since they alone afford the most adequate base for life's full explanation. For a Christian, they also have the basic warrant of revelation.

A. HUMAN RESPONSIBILITY

The first dogma of Christianity is that *man is a responsible being*. It asserts this in spite of three serious objections which may be raised against it:

> I did not come into this world by choice; why then should I accept responsibility for my life?

> I am but part of a whole, subject to the same physical and chemical laws that govern stones, subject to the some physiological and biological laws that govern animals, subject to the same sociological and psychological laws that govern crowds, subject to the same economic laws that govern society; why then should I accept responsibility as an individual?

> I am linked to a whole cosmic process stretching from beyond the years and going on to across the centuries; why then should I accept responsibility for my destiny?

The Christian answer to these objections is in terms of its basic dogma that God is life's final cause. (The term "final cause" is better than the term "first cause"—for while "final cause" defines God's relation to the world in terms of purpose, the term "first cause" seeks to define it in terms of time. Time is a category that we may not apply to God.) This answer means:

> That I must live my life responsibly, not because life is my choice but because I have a responsible nature. I am created by God in such a way that I am both able to and am expected to live responsibly toward him. "God created man in his own image" (Gen. 1:27).

> That I must accept responsibility as an individual since I am an individual to God. He thinks of me as me. It is as an individual that I stand before my Maker. He is my Father. "Not one [sparrow] will fall to the ground without your Father's will" (Matt. 10:29; cf. Luke 12:6).

> That I must accept responsibility for my destiny because my destiny depends in the final analysis not on any cosmic process but on my individual response to God's activity: an activity which is cosmic in scope, but which also at the same time is directed toward each individual separately. He "loved me and gave himself for me" (Gal. 2:20).

In Buddhism, this dogma of human responsibility is stated within the context of the doctrine of *kamma*. Just as in Christianity, God is the final point of orientation for all other dogmas, in Buddhism it is the kammic principle.

> According to the seed that's sown,
>   So is the fruit ye reap therefrom,
> Doer of good will gather good,
>   Doer of evil, evil reaps;
> Sown is the seed, and thou shalt taste
>   The fruit thereof.
>   *(Sanyutta Nikaya)*

Stripped of all its embroidery, the doctrine of *kamma* asserts:

> That I am responsible for what I am, since life is not haphazard but is determined by a principle of justice, each condition of life being the result of its own deserts.

> That *kamma* is produced by action consciously willed, so

that while *kamma* is a cosmic law, it is also the law of my own being. It means that I am master of my destiny.

That also I share in the *kamma* of others, and they share in mine. In being born into a particular environment, I become part of the result of the *kamma* of others as they are part of mine. Thus the kammic law includes the fact that I can share my deserts, others partaking of the results of my action.[1]

Thus stated in its bareness, we find that the theory of *kamma* not only teaches the fact of human responsibility but also shows that the human situation in which that responsibility is exercised is a particular kind of situation.

First of all, *it is an ethical situation*. The emphasis in the theory of *kamma* is on moral action. The ethical elements in man's situation are singled out as primary.

Second, *it is a given situation*. The theory of *kamma* refuses to give any explanation of origins. It simply describes the situation in which man is and with which he has to deal.

Third, *it is a personal situation*. There is no chance of shifting responsibility for one's personal predicament. Every man is the author of his own *kamma* and reaps the fruit thereof.

Fourth, *it is a shared situation*. *Kamma* does not operate on individuals in isolation. Each individual is bound to his fellows.

This fourfold description of the human situation is the Christian description also, but with this difference: that whereas in Buddhism this situation is that *from which* man must get free, in Christianity it is that *in which* man must find his freedom. This difference between Buddhism and Christianity is fundamental.

How does this difference arise? It arises because, in Buddhism, "death" is a final category. It is the one certain experience of man, the one dependable fact which is independent of man. The kammic situation, therefore, is seen as a circle. It is a cycle re-

---

[1] This sharing of one's deserts is stated to be true in Buddhist teaching in a direct sense also, for *pattidana*—the transference of merit—is set forth as one of the ten moral actions. Thus not only do others share in my good *kamma* because I am part of their environment, but I can also actually transfer merit to them; i.e., they share in *me*.

volving round and round the fact of death, man's true freedom being achieved when he has escaped from this situation.

In Christianity, on the other hand, the final category is life and not death. The result is that the human situation is not seen as a circle but rather as an ascending spiral, man achieving his destiny as he is able to co-operate freely in God's progressive purpose for his world. The Buddhist talks of *sansara,* life's meaningless round; the Christian speaks of the Kingdom of God, life's meaningful ascent.

B. THE KINGDOM OF GOD

We have already said that the basic dogma of Christianity is that *God is life's final cause.* This means not only that man has to accept life with responsibility but also that God deals with life responsibly. He does not stand aside and let the world run its course; he enters into the life of the world and maintains his rule there. They who have eyes to see discern in the world and its life, not the endless becoming and dying which is *sansara,* but the Kingdom of God—his sovereign love and his ruling providence.

It is not necessary to say that this dogma of God's active sovereignty is asserted in the face of life's tragedy. Sorrow and suffering, doubt and disappointment, sin and evil: these are not brushed aside. But, in spite of them, the Christian contends that God reigns, and that he reigns here and now. This means love for the world.

However, this sovereignty of God is a sovereignty of will and not of being. What is asserted is not that God's rule goes without challenge, but that God's rule is maintained effectively in the midst of conflict with evil and with wrong.

Thus the human situation is not fully described until it is made clear that God, too, partakes in that situation. God is an active participant in human life. He works from the inner core of human personality through the lives of those who obey him, working on the stuff of human actions by molding them to a fulfillment of his own purposes, and working also directly and immediately—the divine possibility being therefore never absent in any human situation in spite of man's impotence.

The Buddhist way of freedom is built on the thesis that while, on the one hand, *kamma* is the law that controls and explains the vicissitudes of sansaric existence, this sansaric existence is, on the other hand, false existence, so that when desire (*tanha*), which is what binds us to this existence, is cut, release is obtained from the operations of the kammic principle. This whole position may be summarized for clarity as follows:

> The situation into which I am born is the result of my *kamma*.

> My volitional actions performed without true understanding produce *kamma*.

> Ignorance that the world is impermanent (*anicca*), and that I am without self-identity (*anatta*), and that my bondage is by desire (*tanha*)—these determine my volition. In other words, *kamma* is operative because I live falsely.

> There is no way out of my predicament within the control of *kamma*: all I can do is to improve my lot and the lot of others.

> But when I see that *kamma* is merely the principle that operates in the world as I have misunderstood it, and that life rightly understood is not governed by *kamma* but by *dhamma,* then I am free.

Christianity, in contrast, since it accepts this life with all its vicissitudes as truly life, a gift from God in which God lives with us, refuses to allow that freedom can consist in any form of escape from this life. We cannot assert the fact of human responsibility and at the same time seek a salvation that denies that responsibility! Besides, how can the principle of *kamma* be true, and yet be true only of a false type of existence? Must we not rather believe that since God and his activity are part of the human situation, these come within the operation of the principle of *kamma* instead of being an exception to it, so that salvation is brought to man because of the very inclusiveness of the kammic principle? The Christian position is that, on the one hand, God paid and pays the price of being involved with man in the human situation; and that, on the other hand, man reaps the benefit of this action of God. One way of describing Christian salvation is to describe it as the result of *pattidana,* man enjoying the merits of God's loving and holy action in Jesus Christ.

Thus the principle of *kamma* is the principle within which salvation is wrought, and not that from which salvation has to be obtained. The inconsistency of Buddhist teaching in postulating exceptions to the kammic principle is simply the result of viewing life from the point of view of death and not from the point of view of God. Once God is ruled out, death becomes the boundary of life.

> Be not mocked!
> Life which ye prize is long drawn agony:
> Only its pains abide; its pleasures are
>   As birds which light and fly.
> Ask of the sick, the mourners, ask of him
>   Who tottereth on his staff, lone and forlorn,
> "Liketh thee life?"—these say the babe is wise
>   That weepeth, being born.
>   (*The Light of Asia,* Bk. 8)

This is not true. Life is not slow death. It is not the endless going round of *sansara.* Life is the realm of God's sovereign sway, the satisfying experience of God's love.

C. THE WAY OF SALVATION

What then is the *dhamma,* the truth by which man may be saved, the truth by which man may come to live in this life within God's Kingdom? For that is what salvation is, not something to be attained beyond death, but a way of life now—power for present tasks, purpose for life's responsibility—a life lived within its right context and from the right perspective. The Kingdom of God is a present fact, and to live as a citizen of that Kingdom is a present experience. The third dogma of Christianity, therefore, is concerned with pointing out where God's Kingdom can be certainly discerned and how one may enter into it. What this dogma affirms is that *Jesus is God's act on man's behalf* whereby the nature of God's rule in the world has become manifest and the way of man's salvation laid open. In other words, the *dhamma,* the truth by which man may attain salvation, is not an imperative but an indicative, an affirmation not of what man should do but of what God has already done for man.

Many objections can be raised against this dogma since it is so particularistic. Even when it is granted that it is God who saves, why must any man believe that God, in order to save him, went all the way round to Abraham and began there? Why did God choose that particular race, that particular time, that particular place, and that particular person? The Christian answer is factual. It simply says: "It is so." We cannot give reasons as to why God chose to act in a particular way; all we can do is to try and understand the full consequences and implications of his actions. After all, what is important for us is to apprehend the nature of the salvation he has wrought for us without speculating as to why he adopted the methods he did.

What then are the consequences of God's act in Jesus? In order that we may understand the answer to this question in the light of the *Buddha-dhamma,* let us first look at what that *dhamma* teaches. In it we have a way set forth by which life and the desire for life can be conquered. Life is seen to be at the mercy of death, and death is seen to be able to inflict pain and sorrow on life in three directions.

First, there is *the will to love* which is an essential expression of life. But love merely extends the area of my life, exposing me the more to death's attack. What I love will also die and I shall suffer. Hence the will to love must be dealt with through a life of ascetic discipline[2] and unselfish service. I must do what is *kusala,* meritorious actions which are self-denying and other-regarding.

Second, there is *the will to power* which is also an essential expression of life. This intensifies my sense of self, thus making the impact of death the more terrible. Hence the will to power must also be dealt with through a life of strict morality, in which

---

[2] Asceticism is preparation for death; renunciation is anticipation of death. The principle of Buddhist living is asceticism and not renunciation. To be an ascetic is so to live that when death comes it may not find me hankering for life.

the governing principle should be *ahimsa,* the refusal to inflict needless pain on others and the refusal to exploit others for my own ends.

Third, there is *the will to live* itself, that hankering for life which gives to death its real sting. Hence this will to live too must be dealt with. This is something that can be done only as one is able to deny the very existence of the self.

> No need hath such to live as ye name life;
>> That which began in him when he began
> Is finished: he hath wrought the purpose through
>> Of what did make him Man.
>>> (*Light of Asia,* Bk. 8)

This is the *Buddha-dhamma.*

But what does Christianity teach? One can almost say that it teaches this same *dhamma* from a new perspective and in a new context. For according to the Christian dogma, God is life's point of orientation, and his action in Jesus is determinative for life's meaning. We may state the position formally as follows:

First, since God has loved man in Jesus, *man's will to love* which seeks the self's increase is satisfied, for God's love gives value to man's self. But, at the same time, man is humbled because God's love is so undeserved. This experience of humiliation affords the surest ground for the life of ascetic discipline and other-regarding service.

Second, since God has loved man in Jesus, *man's will to power* which makes for the intensity of the self is also satisfied, for God's love offers to men the privilege of sonship, thus giving them the exhilaration of sharing in his power and his work. But, at the same time, man's will to power is broken, since partnership with God involves fellowship in his sufferings. *Ahimsa* is the refusal to inflict pain; sonship goes further and commits one to sharing pain.

Third, since God has loved man in Jesus, *man's will to live* which is the self's inner craving is also satisfied, for God's love enfranchises the self into God's Kingdom. At the same time, the hankering for existence as such is shattered since now "to live is Christ . . . to die is gain" (Phil. 1:21).

In other words, the Christian message is this: that God has so acted for man in Jesus that life is both denied and affirmed at the same time, man finding in God's love both the stabilizing and the shattering of his personality.

D. THE REDEEMED STATE

"After this I looked, and behold, a great multitude which no man could number, from every nation, from all tribes and peoples and tongues, standing before the throne and before the Lamb, clothed in white robes, with palm branches in their hands, and crying out with a loud voice, 'Salvation belongs to our God who sits upon the throne, and to the Lamb!' . . . 'Who are these, clothed in white robes and whence have they come?' . . . 'These are they who . . . have washed their robes and made them white in the blood of the Lamb'" (Rev. 7:9-10, 13, 14).

In this Christian picture of the redeemed state the central conception is that of a white-robed multitude, the whiteness of their robes being the result of a washing. We have already seen how that in the Christian faith salvation is seen to be the result of God's act in Jesus, so that what is called "washing" is merely the cleansing result on one's life of this deed of God. How does this cleansing take place? It takes place through the plunging of one's life into God's life and action, so that thereafter one lives one's life within his.

It is this idea which is symbolized in the church's act of baptism. It is by this act that a person becomes a member of the church, the formula used being: I baptize you in "the name of the Father and of the Son and of the Holy Spirit"[3] (Matt. 28:19). The word "baptize" means to plunge into. So that this is what is symbolized: that the act of becoming a Christian is an act by which one begins to live within a new environment and under new standards of reference and subject to new influences. When I am baptized, I am plunged into the life of God to live there ever after.

But there is a further consequence of baptism besides the cleansing and healing that comes by this investing of life with a

---

[3] See later for the significance of this threefold description of God. The word "name" in this formula means "personality."

new meaning and a new context. It is the consequence of removing from life its natural boundary, that of death. As one begins to share in life's new meaning, death becomes increasingly irrelevant. It is seen to be only an incident in one's earthly life and not an incident at all in the life of God's Kingdom. Thus it loses its sting. It has no more power to dissolve life, for where life has been lived according to God's purpose it has an eternal quality in itself. Death cannot destroy life which is already eternal life—the life lived in God. Neither can death corrupt life's true achievements.

In other words, in the redeemed state there is not only a real salvation of life—there is also a true conquest of death. In God's Kingdom, which stretches beyond death, everything that in earthly life has been of real value is garnered. This is the fourth dogma of Christianity, its dogma about death, its assertion that *death has been destroyed.*

It is a difficult assertion to believe in and maintain in spite of death's continued toll, but it remains the one dogma to which the Christian spirit inevitably turns and which it always finds to be true when death arrives. For when death arrives, the Christian does know that "underneath are the everlasting arms" (Deut. 33:27; cf. John 11:25; 1 Cor. 15:54-55; Rev. 21:4).

To attain *nibbana* is to be rid of the sorrow and meaninglessness of life's constant becoming; to attain unto Life Eternal is to attain to the state where *nibbana* itself is fulfilled in the deathless perfecting of life's meaning.

PART II:
THAT YOU MAY BELIEVE

"Truly, truly, I say to you, unless one is born anew, he cannot see the kingdom of God. . . . That which is born of the flesh is flesh, and that which is born of the Spirit is spirit. Do not marvel that I said to you, 'You must be born anew.' The wind blows where it wills, and you hear the sound of it, but you do not know whence it comes or whither it goes; so it is with every one who is born of the Spirit." . . . For God sent the Son into the world not to condemn the world, but that the world might be saved through him.

(John 3:3, 6-8, 17)

3.
The Christian Faith

ANICCA: *Behind every blossoming forth*
there is a fading, behind every
attainment a loss, behind every
*life death.**

ONE need there is above all needs—it is the need to know
life's meaning.

I live—yes—but is life itself significant? What if I choose not
to live? But suicide is an offense against the state; each life means
one extra citizen. But surely every citizen is not an asset to the
state, and even when one is an asset, the question is not primarily
what my life means to someone else, but what life itself means—
my life, the life of others, the life of the state itself.

As I look at life, my life, and life in general, one fact is self-
evident—the fact of change. Nothing is permanent. The grass
withers; the flowers fade; the sun sets; people die. Even every
achievement of man is touched with mortality. What is progressive today is obscurantist tomorrow. Kingdoms rise and fall; peoples wax and wane. Life goes on constantly changing, and for
every man certainly ending in death. "All flesh is grass, and all its
beauty is like the flower of the field" (Isa. 40:6).

Has life no meaning then except that it is here and that I have
to live it? But why "have to"? Because life is able to arouse a
craving for itself in all who live, and no one really does want to
commit suicide. That means, then, that life has no meaning except as something to be surpassed, and that I must learn to live
without the craving to live, live without attachment to life!

---
* *Sanyutta Nikaya.*

But that is only half the truth, the half which we can see when we look at life from within itself: there is another half, the half whose truth is outside this life and to which this life is a negative witness. ". . . for the things that are seen are transient, but the things that are unseen are eternal" (2 Cor. 4:18).

The quality of *anicca* is proof of life's meaninglessness, but it is also proof that life has a meaning in that which is eternal. *Anicca* is the sign of meaninglessness; *nicca* is the sign of meaning. But nothing is *nicca*—no, nothing—except the craving for life: and what if the truth be that that craving is meant to be satisfied and not destroyed! Is not the existence of craving proof of the existence of the source of its satisfaction? "Blessed are you that hunger now, for you shall be satisfied" (Luke 6:21).

One solution of life's problem is to seek to destroy its craving because life is *anicca;* another solution is to seek the satisfaction of that craving in that which is *nicca.* The first solution is an attempt to escape meaninglessness; the second solution is an attempt to find meaning. Indeed, the two solutions are interdependent, for it is only as the craving for that which is *anicca* is destroyed that the self is willing to seek that which is *nicca.* "For whoever would save his life will lose it; and whoever loses his life . . . will save it" (Mark 8:35).

What then is life's meaning? Life cannot yield it; it must be brought into life. It is like bringing meaning into heaps of stones and sand and cement and timber. Their meaning is not in themselves; their meaning is not even in the men who handle them. They get meaning when they are brought within the purposes of an architect and are related together in a building. So it is with life.

Life is stuff with which lives are built. It has no meaning in itself. Neither can we give it meaning except meanings which are temporary. If it is truly to receive meaning, we who live must first find meaning ourselves by being related to a purpose that is eternal, a purpose outside ourselves, a purpose outside life itself, a purpose which can exist only in the ground of all life, in life's final cause. "The grass withers, and the flower falls, but the word of the Lord abides for ever" (1 Peter 1:24-25).

A. LIFE ETERNAL

The first datum, then, of the Christian faith is this, that there is *Life Eternal*.[1] The affirmations of this datum may be stated as follows:

> The solution of life's intrinsic problem must be made in terms of meaning rather than meaninglessness.
>
> Life's meaning is found in God who is life's final cause.
>
> Life, as we know it, is meant to be lived in relation to him and his purposes.
>
> So do our lives become *nicca,* partaking in God's life itself.
>
> "In him was life, and the life was the light of men" (John 1:4).

> DUKKHA: *One thing only do I teach,*
> *O brothers, sorrow and*
> *deliverance from sorrow.**

TWO ways there are in which we can live in this impermanent world.

We may live as desiring the world or as renouncing it, as wishing to enjoy it or as running away from it. But neither way is really satisfactory, for both ways are dogged by sorrow. He who sets himself to enjoy the world finds that he cannot keep the things which he enjoys for they are impermanent. "Do not lay up for yourselves treasures on earth, where moth and rust consume and where thieves break in and steal" (Matt. 6:19). Nor is it possible to keep one's sense of pleasure once attained, for such pleasure soon turns to the pain of a desire for more. "Every one who drinks of this water will thirst again" (John 4:13).

---

1 The primary connotation of the term "Life Eternal" is not endless life. It is endless simply because it is eternal in the first place. Endless life is life lived within the time category; though, as if it were, time is transcended horizontally. Eternal life means that time is transcended vertically, or, in other words, life is lifted to a new plane where it is lived undetermined by temporal and temporary considerations. In terms of the background of Jewish thought, eternal life means the life that belongs to God's age, so that eternal life begins when one begins to live in terms of God's will.
* *Majjhima Nikaya.*

But while this is true, there is no escape from the experience of sorrow along the opposite path either. For the chief weakness about the way of world-renunciation is that the world cannot be so renounced. We are part of the world, and we have the world within us. We can renounce riches, but the struggle with the desire for it still goes on inside us; we can renounce the pleasure of satisfying our appetites, but the appetites remain an aching void within.

The cause of *dukkha* is in the nature of the world and the fact that we are bound to it, so that a life lived in terms of the world, whether we do it positively or negatively, is still a life lived within its bondage. The cure of *dukkha* can come only by walking a middle path, a path between the two extremes of indulgence and renunciation, the path of discipline, of asceticism.[2] "If your right eye causes you to sin, pluck it out . . . if your right hand causes you to sin, cut it off . . ." (Matt. 5:29-30).

But then is it not true that, to live in any sense at all adequately, we must live *en rapport* with our environment? We cannot just live a life of discipline. Life wilts unless it is spontaneous in some degree, and unless in some measure it finds its environment natural so that it can take it for granted.

We dare not take the world for granted, however, and live naturally and spontaneously in it, for it is a world of *dukkha*. As far as this world is concerned we must live the life of discipline. It is in the other world, the world-eternal, which is the natural world of our lives, that we can live spontaneously. In this world we are pilgrims; it is of the other world that we are children. Here we live ascetically; there we are free. ". . . our commonwealth is in heaven . . ." (Phil. 3:20).

Meaningful living, then, is to live *en rapport* with the purposes of God for us and for the world. It is to live *en rapport* with God's life. But, and this is where the real problem lies, we do not live naturally in God. Our nature is warped and diseased. The world is inside us and part of us in such a way as to make it impossible

---

2 *Askesis* = exercise, training. The attitude of renunciation is an attitude toward the world. It sees the world as evil. The attitude of asceticism, however, is an attitude toward the self. It sees the self as in need of discipline.

for us to live spontaneously in God's world. God's presence causes us pain, and our natural reaction to him is one of rejection.

". . . the whole world is in the power of the evil one" (1 John 5:19). Until and unless this evil is dealt with, both in the world and in us, there is no final solution to the problem of living. For life's basic ill is not *dukkha* but *doha*[3]—that attitude of rebellion and disloyalty which we have toward God who is the ground of our being, the final cause of the world, and the purpose which gives meaning to life.

The cause of *dukkha* is my clinging to self; it is this same self-centeredness which is also the cause of *doha:* the unconscious or conscious assumption that I hold within myself the clue to life's meaning and can of myself discover and obey that clue. *Dukkha* comes as a result of the self's craving to satisfy itself with the things of this world; *doha* comes as a result of the self's attempt at self-satisfaction. The fruit seems good to eat; it also brings the promise that we shall be as God (Gen. 3:5-6).

It is not enough, therefore, that I seek to walk in the middle path—the path of discipline—nor is my first need for a teacher who will teach me that path. My need rather is for a savior who will do for me what I cannot do for myself, who will take away from me that twist in my nature so that I can come to live naturally and spontaneously in God. It is I who am the problem and not the world; it is my *doha* and not the world's *dukkha* that needs primary solution.

B. A NEW CREATION

So we come to the second datum of the Christian faith: *a new creation*. The affirmations of this datum may be stated as follows:

I am by nature unnatural, standing in need of healing and wholeness.

God has provided for that healing
   (1) by revealing to me the sickness of my own nature,

---

[3] The meaning of the word "sin" in Christian teaching is so complex that it is difficult to use one word to denote it. In this book I have preferred the word *"doha"* to *"papa."*

thus leading me to repentance, to a change of mind about myself;

(2) by showing me what true life is as lived in him, thus leading me to prayer, to an earnest desire for that life for myself;

(3) by offering this life to me in himself, thus leading me to faith, to that life of fellowship with him which is life eternal.

"Therefore, if any one is in Christ, he is a new creation" (2 Cor. 5:17).

SARANA: *Be your own light, be
your own refuge. Let
the truth be your light
and your refuge.**

THREE gifts God has given to men whereby men may be saved.

First, there is the gift of himself. He entered into responsive fellowship with one of the peoples whom he had made, the Jews, that through them all men may come to know him and themselves. ". . . by you," God said to Abraham, the father of the Jews, "all the families of the earth shall bless themselves" (Gen. 12:3).

Through the obedience that he wrought among this people whom he chose, he became known in the lives of their saints and the words of their prophets. He led them from a dim discerning of his nature to a true understanding of himself as the only God, one without a second, whose will was holy and without compromise, and whose love was limitless and without sentiment. "I am the LORD . . . you shall have no other gods before me" (Exod. 20:2-3).

Against this background, gradually apprehended, there became manifest the real dimensions of sin, of *doha,* of that disloyalty to God which is man's moral disease. The Jews as a nation, in spite of the pious among them, refused to worship God alone

---

* *Parinibbana Sutta.*

and for himself. They sought to combine his worship with the
worship of material prosperity. Neither would they measure themselves against his holy will; they sought rather to reduce that will
into workable proportions. Nor would they respond in glad aban-
don to God's love; they sought instead to exploit that love as
meaning privilege for them.

". . . but where sin increased, grace abounded all the more"
(Rom. 5:20). God himself came, born as a man, as a Jew. He
lived a human life; he carried a human name (he was called
Jesus); and men saw in him what true life was. This life he
offered to them also, teaching them that it could be lived if only
men would live in fellowship with him.

He showed himself to be life's master. He healed the sick;
he raised the dead. He brought joy to the sorrowing, release for
the suffering, and a new beginning to spoiled lives. He "dwelt
among us, full of grace and truth; we have beheld his glory"
(John 1:14). Only a few, however, responded to his invitation
to live in fellowship with him, while many simply thought of
him as a revolutionary purveyor of cheap religion.

When religion itself is under the control of man's moral disease,
when man in his *doha* seeks to bring God himself within the
ambit of his own self-seeking, then God must either come to
terms with man or be put away. So was Jesus put away, because
he would not serve the ambitions or designs of men. So also did
God deal finally with sin.

In seeking to pit itself against God, sin has to throw away its
every disguise and come out in the open. It is seen for what it is.
It has also to meet God on God's own level—for he never un-
bends—and on that level sin has to match itself against God's
utter mercy. Thus are men turned in repentance from themselves
to God, asking to walk with him in loyal fellowship rather than
live with themselves in the loneliness of their ingratitude. In
allowing man to do with him as he wished, God did for man what
man could not do for himself—he came to grips with sin. He
"made a public example of them, triumphing over them in [the
cross]" (Col. 2:15).

God's second gift to man is the gift of his will. For God's

fellowship with man is an abiding and a continuing fellowship. We are not left simply with a history of God's dealing with the Jews, a history from which we may draw lessons for ourselves. We are not left simply with the example of Jesus, a life lived long ago, an example which we may seek to imitate. God's offer rather is that we may live with him in day-to-day fellowship, knowing and loving and doing his will. His will is the *dhamma,* the *dhamma* for us, the *dhamma* for the world.

We come to know this will through the Risen Christ, for just as Jesus lived in Palestine, a man among men, so is Jesus alive now on earth, inviting us as he invited the men of his day to live with him in daily companionship. They saw him with their naked eyes—we don't—but we know nevertheless that he is here. His own promise and the witness of countless persons through the ages are sufficient proof. He is with us "always, to the close of the age" (Matt. 28:20).

Thus is God's will revealed to us: the Risen Christ interpreting for us God's past dealings with the Jews, and indeed with all men. We know his will as we accompany Jesus in imaginative understanding through those years of his earthly ministry. We know it as we respond to the bidding of Christ risen, challenging us to a life of discipleship. We know it also as we abide in the fellowship of those who with us seek to do his will.

And that is God's third gift to us—the gift of his church, the *sangha* of them that believe. In this society is the final undoing of our *doha,* for here we cease to be alone and to count as only one. We are limbs of a body. Also because God's purpose for this body is so high and holy, we are saved from self-satisfaction in the humbling knowledge that neither we in ourselves nor as members of his body even approximate to that purpose. It is, as we take our membership in the body of Christ seriously, that we are saved from ourselves and our pride. Besides in this body is the constant miracle of fellowship, God's gift to men through his Spirit, a gift which men most need but constantly sin against. "And all who believed were together and had all things in common . . . And day by day, attending the temple together and breaking bread in their homes, they partook of food with glad and generous hearts, praising God and having favor with all the people. . . . And with great power the apostles gave their testimony to the resurrection of the Lord Jesus, and great grace was upon them all" (Acts 2:44, 46-47; 4:33).

C. THE DIVINE FELLOWSHIP

Thus can be stated a third datum of the Christian faith: *the divine fellowship*. The affirmations of this datum may be formulated as follows:

In the discipline and life of the church, constantly nourished by the fellowship of God's Spirit, is our salvation—our *sarana* in the *sangha*.

In glad obedience to God's abiding will, revealed and ratified in Jesus, and ever made accessible to us through the Risen Christ, is our salvation—our *sarana* in the *dhamma*.

In the cleansing acceptance of God's love, revealing us to ourselves and himself to us, and causing us to love him more than ourselves, is our salvation—our *sarana* in the living God.

"For God so loved the world that he gave his only Son, that whoever believes in him should not perish but have eternal life" (John 3:16).[4]

ANATTA: *Is it justifiable to*
think of these which
are impermanent—
this is mine; this am I;
this is my soul?*

FOUR truths every man must realize about himself:

1. The truth of self.
2. The truth of the ground of self.

4 That which is given in this chapter is necessarily a condensed summary of the Christian story. Indeed in many ways it is only a statement of the meaning of that story. Those who are unacquainted with the details of the story must, therefore, read it for themselves. For a first understanding, it will be enough to read some short history of the Old Testament, St. Mark's Gospel, and the Acts of the Apostles.

* From the Second Discourse of the Buddha—The Buddha-Dhamma by Narada Thera.

3. The truth of the salvation of self.
4. The truth of the means of the self's salvation.

No description of a person's religious situation is complete until it has taken seriously and dealt adequately with what a person really is. What am I? I share in the world's *anicca*. I change, I decay, I will die. I am never the same at any moment, and as far as I know I have no identity in myself. My sense of identity seems only to be the result of the fact that the stream of fleeting moments which make me up is distinguishable from other streams. Besides, I also share in the composite nature of all things. Like everything else I too am made of parts, and like everything else I too must come to dissolution. Indeed, there is no "I" which I can perceive which is immortal when all life is mortal, which is eternal when all life is impermanent, which is identical when all life is changing, which is unique when all life is composite. Man is like a passing breath; his days are like a flitting shadow (Job 7:7; 8:9).

And yet surely this is only true of me as I know myself. As I know myself I know only the *skandhas*—the complex of sensations, ideas, thoughts, emotions, and volitions! But then there is another "I" myself, as God knows me and as he has made me. For God has made me in his own image; that is, as a self-conscious person able to share in God's life and reflect God's character.

To be made in God's image means that I am so made as to be capable of response to God so that I may live by that response, his image in me being not a replica but a reflection, something that is in me because of God's continuing relation with me.

Thus while as a creature I am altogether a creature, possessing nothing which in its own nature is *nicca;* yet, in that God enters into relationship with me as part of his act of creating me, I come to receive immortality. In other words, I am *anatta* in myself; it is God's relationship with me which constitutes me as *atta*. Abraham lives because God is the God of Abraham: and God is not the God of the dead but of the living (Mark 12:26-27).

That God establishes relationship with me is, however, only a preliminary truth; there is the further question as to how I react to that relationship and how God deals with my reaction. Shall I serve God or use him? Accept him or reject him? My natural inclination is to reject him completely or, if possible, to use him, to fit him into my scheme of life. This is my *doha* against the ground of my real being. But even so, God does not leave me alone. He pursues me with love; he chastises me with justice. He keeps me bound to his world, the world eternal. It is by this continuing decision of God with respect to me that I keep my immortality; so also do I receive identity and uniqueness. I remain "I" before God. ". . . the LORD appeared to me from afar," saying, "I have loved you with an everlasting love; therefore I have continued my faithfulness to you" (Jer. 31:3).

But may not God refuse to undergird my being with his love, and if I persist in the attitude of *doha* toward him, will I not receive from him a final condemnation? God forbid! And yet I know that my immortality is dependent on God's decision, and that it behooves me to "fear him who can destroy both soul and body" (Matt. 10:28). So that the real question for me is not what God will do, but what I shall do. If I persist in my *doha,* then the curse of *dukkha* haunts my whole life. I have *dukkha* in my earthly existence; I have greater *dukkha* in my relationship with the eternal. But if I repent, and change my attitude to myself and to God, accepting the threefold gift which he offers me, then I have peace—in my earthly life the peace which the world cannot take away whatever be life's *dukkha,* and in my experience of eternal life peace itself.

D. THE GIFT OF IMMORTALITY

A fourth datum of the Christian faith, therefore, will be: *the gift of immortality*. The affirmations of this datum can be set forth as follows:

I am a creature, completely so; and there is no part of me which is other than human.

I am also a creature created in God's image, possessing a

nature that can reflect God and therefore possessing also his reflection, God himself maintaining the relationship which makes this possible.[5]

It is this relationship between God and me which is the basis of my *amata*—my transcendence over death.

God wills this gift of immortality to be received along with and for the sake of his other gift—the gift of salvation.

"For thou dost not give me up to Sheol, or let thy godly one see the Pit" (Ps. 16:10).

---

5 The common idea that man is made up of a mortal body and an immortal soul is Greek in origin. From the Bible point of view we speak of man's soul when we speak of him in his relation to God. The soul is the whole person (Gen. 2:7) as related to God. When it is said that God made man in his own image, we must understand the reference to include both man's particular nature as well as his Godward relation which is part of that nature. God's image in man is not something that belongs to man's nature as such. Rather it is something that belongs to man's nature in its Godward relation.

4.

The Christian Life

SILA: *Cease to do evil;*
learn to do good;
cleanse your own heart;
this is the religion of
*the Buddhas.**

FIVE disciplines pertain to a life lived truly. How can we reflect God's image if our lives are like troubled waters? And if we do not reflect his image, how shall we say that we live the true life of the soul? We must, therefore, seek to maintain in daily living the peace that we receive from God when we enter into the life of salvation. This is not to say that our lives can ever be free in this world of the strain and stress of living, but that such strain and stress should not and need not destroy the peace which God gives. ". . . in me," says Jesus, "you may have peace. In the world you have tribulation; but be of good cheer, I have overcome the world" (John 16:33).

A. DISCIPLINE

The problem of *sila,* of moral living, is the same as the problem of *saddha,* of religious living. In both cases the problem is caused by our natural tendency to *doha,* to disloyalty to the ground of our being caused by the assumption of self-sufficiency. In the religious life, when this *doha* is acknowledged and renounced we have fellowship with God, and this fellowship, constantly maintained, destroys also the effects of our *doha* on all life's relationships. "And the peace of God . . . will keep your hearts and your minds in Christ Jesus" (Phil. 4:7).

---

* The Buddha-Dhamma by Narada Thera.

The effects of *doha* in our life-relationships can be seen in the acts of *doha* which we do against our fellows. We tend to forget that they too receive their selves from God, and that they too belong to God as uniquely as we. Just as before our salvation we sought to use God for our own purposes, so now, even though we have entered into fellowship with God, the tendency persists to use others and to think of others as those whom we may use. Indeed, even the tendency to use God persists. It is against these tendencies that we have to maintain rigid discipline, a control not only over our actions but also over our minds and our wills, taking "every thought captive to obey Christ" (2 Cor. 10: 5).

The tendency to sin against the personality of our fellows expresses itself in five main ways:

Pansil[1]

1. Anger and strife and all that leads to the taking of another's life. "You have heard that it was said to men of old, 'You shall not kill; and whoever kills shall be liable to judgment.' But I say to you that every one who is angry with his brother shall be liable to judgment; whoever insults his brother shall be liable to the council, and whoever says, 'You fool!' shall be liable to the hell of fire" (Matt. 5:21-22).

2. Every form of dishonesty, the taking of things that are not ours. "Let the thief no longer steal, but rather let him labor, doing honest work with his hands, so that he may be able to give to those in need" (Eph. 4:28). "Take heed, and beware of all covetousness; for a man's life does not consist in the abundance of his possessions" (Luke 12:15).

3. Indulgence in sensuality, the lustful violation of another's person. "You have heard that it was said, 'You shall not commit adultery.' But I say to you that every one who looks at a woman lustfully has already committed adultery with her in his heart. If your right eye causes you to sin, pluck it out and throw it

---

1 Murder, dishonesty, sensuality, lying, and drunkenness are the five classic Hindu and Buddhist categories of wrongdoing. For a Buddhist, taking *pansil* seems to have the same emotive value as the taking of Holy Communion for a Christian.

away; it is better that you lose one of your members than that your whole body be thrown into hell" (Matt. 5:27-29).

4. Deceit, lying, slander, the malicious robbing of another's good name. "Therefore, putting away falsehood, let every one speak the truth with his neighbor, for we are members one of another. . . . Let no evil talk come out of your mouths, but only such as is good for edifying, as fits the occasion, that it may impart grace to those who hear. . . . Let all bitterness and wrath and anger and clamor and slander be put away from you, with all malice, and be kind to one another, tenderhearted, forgiving one another, as God in Christ forgave you" (Eph. 4:25, 29, 31-32).

5. Drunkenness and passion and all that leads to moral insensibility. "Be sober, be watchful. Your adversary the devil prowls around like a roaring lion, seeking some one to devour. Resist him, firm in your faith. . . . And . . . the God of all grace, who has called you to his eternal glory in Christ, will himself restore, establish, and strengthen you. To him be the dominion for ever and ever. Amen" (1 Peter 5:8-11).

The saved life is a life of *sila,* for salvation makes ethics obligatory. It also makes it possible. Indeed, were men challenged to live the ethical life without being endued also with the power to do it, their situation would be desperate. But in the Christian faith ethical living is demanded as the fruit of the experience of God's saving act. *Sila* is not in order to merit salvation; it is rather the result of having entered into the experience of salvation already.

". . . you have put off the old nature with its practices and have put on the new nature, which is being renewed in knowledge after the image of its creator" (Col. 3:9-10).

> SAMADHI: *The truth remains hidden*
> *from him whom desire*
> *and hate absorb.**

SIX attitudes must be habitual to the self, if the discipline of *sila* is to be really fruitful.

For the peace of the saved life is both discipline and spon-

---

* *Vinaya Mahavagga.*

taneity, both a war against *doha* and an expression of true *samadhi*.
Samadhi means that the self is in its right situation.

1. Unfettered by *tanha*, free of its craving for this life;
2. released from *avijja*, knowing what true life is;
3. set in the way of *metta*, the way of loving-kindness;
4. sharing with God his *karuna*, his suffering compassion for others;
5. in all things with *mudita*, joy abundant;
6. and kept in the way of *upekkha*, the untroubled peace of a soul at rest in God.

B. LOVE

As is evident, the key to this attitude of the self is love. Only the love of persons can destroy the craving for things. Only love can give true perspective to life. Only love can lead us into a life of costly service. Love alone will keep us rejoicing and shedding joy when service brings suffering in its train. Indeed it is the one thing that will keep the soul at rest, for love is of God.

> If I speak in the tongues of men and of angels, but have not love, I am a noisy gong or a clanging cymbal. And if I have prophetic powers, and understand all mysteries and all knowledge, and if I have all faith, so as to remove mountains, but have not love, I am nothing. If I give away all I have, and if I deliver my body to be burned, but have not love, I gain nothing.

Whether *buddhi* or *nana, iddhi* or *dana*, or even *tapo*—these are of no profit, if the self is not tranquilized in love.

> Love is patient and kind; love is not jealous or boastful; it is not arrogant or rude. Love does not insist on its own way; it is not irritable or resentful; it does not rejoice at wrong, but rejoices in the right. Love bears all things, believes all things, hopes all things, endures all things.
> Love never ends (1 Cor. 13:1-8).

But can we love? We can, if only we will keep ourselves in

true *samadhi,* bringing our souls to rest in the one certain fact of our existence, God's love for us. "In this is love, not that we loved God but that he loved us and sent his Son" (1 John 4:10). So that the *samadhi* of the self is attained not by concentrating attention on our duty to love as by bringing the mind to meditate on the whole range of God's love for us—its length and breadth, its height and depth (Eph. 3:18). The *jhana* that can really bring to an end the egocentricity of the self is *jhana* of the self's absolute dependence on God's love not only for its well-being, but for its being itself. The love of God is both the basis of self and its solvent.[2]

Love for our fellows is simply the grateful reflection in our lives of God's love for us, the spontaneous expression of our lives lived in their true relations. The source of love is not in us but in God, and if love goes from us, it is simply because it is flowing through us. Let this, therefore, be our constant meditation, our *jhana:*

that we are *anicca,* impermanent, apart from God;
that we are *anatta,* soulless, apart from him;
that it is his love which dissolves our *dukkha,* our sorrow;
that it is his love which is our *sarana,* our refuge;
that without him we can keep no *sila,* no virtue;
and that in the remembrance of his love is our true *samadhi,*
our rest.

"This is my body which is given for you. Do this in remembrance of me" (Luke 22:19).

PANNA: *The Perfect One is free
from every theory, for the
Perfect One has seen.**

---

2 In the New Testament, the primary word for love is *"agape,"* and *agape* means a love that is spontaneous and uncaused. It is only God who loves in this way. Our love to God is a response to God's love toward us. Thus Paul, who is accurate in his use of words, practically always uses the word "faith" and not "love" to denote man's response to God's love. As for man's love to fellowman, Paul uses the word "love," since he wants to teach that one man's love toward another is but God's love to that man through the other man.

* The Essence of the Buddha's Teaching by Nyanatiloka.

SEVEN steps mark the way of the self's response to God's love. It is the self's necessary response, for unless the self does so respond, no amount of theorizing about God's love will help. *Sila* depends on *samadhi; samadhi* depends on *panna. Panna* means true understanding, the understanding which comes as a result of direct vision, the immediate apprehension of truth, the certain knowledge of things and their relations. Such insight can come only as the self actually moves into its right situation, and is therefore able to see things from the right perspective. In other words, the only way of clearing one's vision and attaining to true understanding is to enter into the experience of the vision of God in his total relationship to man.

C. VISION

Such a vision normally comes, and certainly comes, when a man is completely disillusioned about himself and his world, and when in his inmost self he feels the void of life. Abraham saw his vision of God when life had lost all meaning for him among the many gods of his people. Moses saw his vision of God when he felt his own impotence in the face of his great longing to deliver his nation from bondage. Isaiah saw his vision of God when his hopes for his country lay shattered with the death of King Uzziah. Jeremiah saw his vision of God when he felt lost in the winter of the unchecked wickedness of his time. Ezekiel saw his vision of God in the midst of the frustration of a foreign exile. Paul saw his vision of God when he felt defeated by his own attempts to stand justified before his conscience. John saw his vision of God when the great empire of Rome was filling the world's horizon with horror.

It is primarily so, man meeting God in the realization of his own extremity.

And when the vision comes, what then? The soul enters into the full implications of it by a total response. There are seven elements that can be distinguished in such a response, elements all of which are not equally prominent in any given experience, but which nevertheless are all there.

1. *Adoration*

Here the creature bows before the Creator in reverence and in humility, acknowledging the distance that separates him from God. He knows that in himself he is nothing. "And I heard every creature in heaven and on earth and under the earth and in the sea, and all therein, saying, 'To him who sits upon the throne and to the Lamb be blessing and honor and glory and might for ever and ever!' " (Rev. 5:13).

2. *Confession*

Here the sinner comes before his Savior in repentance, acknowledging his acts of disloyalty to God who is the ground of his being and the purpose of his existence. God is seen and adored: and in that vision the self is seen and denied. " 'Woe is me! For I am lost; for I am a man of unclean lips, and I dwell in the midst of a people of unclean lips; for my eyes have seen the King . . . ' And he touched my mouth, and said: 'Behold, this has touched your lips; your guilt is taken away, and your sin forgiven' " (Isa. 6:5, 7).

3. *Thanksgiving*

Here the child comes before his Father with gratitude for being forgiven and accepted in the home, and with gratitude also for all the gifts that make up home. "Blessed be the God and Father of our Lord Jesus Christ, who has blessed us in Christ with every spiritual blessing . . . in the Beloved . . . we have redemption through his blood, the forgiveness of our trespasses, according to the riches of his grace which he lavished upon us. . . . in all wisdom and insight . . . for the praise of his glory" (Eph. 1:3, 6-9, 12).

4. *Petition*

Here the subject comes before his King, making known his wants. It is as his subjects that we come, for even though we are children because of his grace, we may not ourselves presume on that grace. We make known our desires and accept to live according to his will.

Hearken to the sound of my cry,
   my King and my God,
   for to thee do I pray.
O LORD, in the morning thou dost hear my voice;
   in the morning I prepare a sacrifice for thee, and watch.
       (Ps. 5:2-3)

Thou hast put more joy in my heart
   than they have when their grain and wine abound.
In peace I will both lie down and sleep;
   for thou alone, O LORD, makest me dwell in safety.
       (Ps. 4:7-8)

5. *Intercession*

Here the partner comes to his Fellow-Partner, sharing with him the problems and demands of their common enterprise. Servants we are, but he has called us friends and taken us into the fellowship of his ministry. "I do not cease to give thanks for you, remembering you in my prayers, that the God of our Lord Jesus Christ, the Father of glory, may give you a spirit of wisdom and revelation . . . that you may know what is the hope to which he has called you, what are the riches of his glorious inheritance in the saints" (Eph. 1:16-18).

6. *Dedication*

Here the soldier comes before his General to renew his oath of allegiance, to do as he is told, to go where he is sent. The Christian is not bound by rules but by the will of a living God. Our end is not goodness but obedience. "But thanks be to God, that you who were once slaves of sin have become obedient from the heart to the standard of teaching to which you were committed" (Rom. 6:17). ". . . present your bodies as a living sacrifice . . . which is your spiritual worship. . . . that you may prove what is the will of God, what is good and acceptable and perfect" (Rom. 12:1-2).

7. *Silence*

In this silence the soul comes to its rest and to rest in God's love. Here is refreshment for life's daily tasks, the source of strength for the soul's growth into the divine perfection.

Even youths shall faint and be weary,
  and young men shall fall exhausted;
but they who wait for the LORD shall renew their strength,
  they shall mount up with wings like eagles,
they shall run and not be weary,
  they shall walk and not faint.
    (Isa. 40:30-31)

"Come to me . . . and I will give you rest . . . and you will find rest for your souls" (Matt. 11:28-29).

> ARAHAT: *Who has completed the
> journey, who from
> everything is wholly
> free, who has destroyed
> all ties.**

EIGHT aspects, one's life can be divided into, and in all of them must a Christian live worthily.

D. WORTH

The *arahat* is the worthy one who has attained freedom, but what must never be forgotten is that the Christian *arahat* has his worth conferred on him by God. "But to all who received him . . . he gave power to become children of God" (John 1:12). Thus the attainment of a Christian is in virtue of the call with which God has called him and to which he has responded. He was a sinner before the call came; he is a sinner now even though God's call has found him: and yet he is also a saint accounted worthy by God because God is gracious, and treated as righteous because of God's righteousness which is now at work in him. ". . . the gospel . . . is the power of God for salvation to every one who has faith . . . For in it the righteousness of God is revealed through faith for faith" (Rom. 1:16-17).

So then the Christian life is the expression in daily living of a status that God has conferred on a person, a life lived worthily of the worth with which God has invested him. This means that one journey of the self is over—the journey of the self to save itself—and that another journey has begun—the journey of the self to appropriate in its fullness the free gift of God's salvation.

---

* *Dhammapada.*

The appropriation of this gift, however, is not a mystic act; it is done in the ordinary process of living; for, let us remind ourselves again, God's gift of salvation is simply and in the first place this life itself lifted to another plane. *Sila, samadhi, panna*— these are not just gateways to arahatship; they are themselves the marks that one has that experience now.

Here we see the full significance of the consequential nature of the Christian ethic. We are first endowed with worth and then show forth that worth in our living. We first enter into eternal life and then manifest in our thoughts and words and deeds the quality of this determining experience.

We manifest it in *sila*—in (1) right speech, (2) right action, (3) and the right means of earning a livelihood.

We manifest it in *samadhi*—in (4) right effort, (5) right attentiveness, (6) and right concentration.

We manifest it in *panna*—in (7) right understanding (8) and right-mindedness.

Thus is shown in life what the Kingdom of God is, the Kingdom which is "righteousness and peace and joy in the Holy Spirit" (Rom. 14:17).

But this is not all that characterizes the life of the *arahat;* there will be in his life another quality also, the desire to share with others what he knows of God's infinite mercy. Other men's needs are his call, and he becomes to them a witness to the Divine wisdom, one whose life is controlled by the desire to share with others the open mystery of God's mind in his intent to save all men. Only he is a true *arahat.* He is a true son who is also an apostle.

"So we are ambassadors for Christ, God making his appeal through us. We beseech you on behalf of Christ, be reconciled to God" (2 Cor. 5:20).

PART III:
AND BELIEVING HAVE LIFE

For if I preach the gospel, that
gives me no ground for boasting. For
necessity is laid upon me. Woe to me
if I do not preach the gospel! For
if I do this of my own will, I have a
reward; but if not of my own will, I
am entrusted with a commission. What
then is my reward? Just this: that in
my preaching I may make the gospel free
of charge, not making full use of my right
in the gospel.

(1 Cor. 9:16-18)

5.

The Christian Believes

God acts; man acts in response. That is the controlling motif of any presentation of the Christian position with respect to faith and life. But no such presentation is complete until the inverse truth is also stated—that God acts in response to man's need. Man's response to God's action can be a saving response only because God's action was meant to save. It is God's answer to the fact of human sin. Sin and salvation, man's need and God's deed, lie at the heart of the human problem and constitute the core of the Christian proclamation.

The Christian faith is summarized for us Christians in a creed, which is for us both a part of worship and a declaration of belief. It seems to me that, inasmuch as we have already attempted to state the Christian message in language significant for the Buddhist, a presentation of the Christian position from its inverse perspective may profitably be made in terms of the Christian creed. This will help to elucidate the Christian position still further. Indeed, the Christian truth is apprehensible only when it is laid hold of by the whole person and not by the mind only, so that the truest verb for a Christian to use in presenting his faith is the verb "believe." To share this belief, and to live by it, is to have life in Christ's name.

I believe in God the Father Almighty, Maker of heaven and earth.

Therefore I do not believe in sin either as an eternal fact or as self-existent. I cannot allow an ultimate dualism in the world. But neither did God create sin. He is Father. In the Bible, sin is explained as the result of a lust for power in the heavenly places (Rev. 12:7-9); it is on earth, too, the result of a lust for

69

power (Gen. 3:5; 11:4). Hence it is that one of the essential elements of sin is the element of *idolatry*—the attempt to worship gods who are men's creation and therefore less than men (Rev. 9:20).

Thus, we must beware of giving any support to the view held by many that in some ultimate sense God is responsible for sin, that sin is the result of a devil whom God has created, or that it is the result of some eternal principle. We must also seek to distinguish between the acts of sin and sin itself. What must be dealt with in men's lives is sin; sinning is merely the result of servitude to sin (Rom. 6:6). In the New Testament, the word *hamartema* is used for an act of sin, and *hamartia* for sin. When the same word is used for both, it causes confusion.

This distinction is important since conversion means the refusal to serve sin. It is the rooting out of the love of sin, and daily contending with its power that still remains over us. He that is born of God does not persist in sinning (1 John 3:9).

The essence of sin, then, lies in its relation to God. The Tamil and Sinhalese word (*papam*) used to translate *hamartema* and *hamartia* is weak because it does not express any Godward relation. Sin is an offense against God's sovereignty, against his almightiness. It is *virodham* rather than *papam*, an act of rebellion and not simply a condition of guilt. Salvation from sin consists in the sole worship of God (Matt. 4:10).

Negatively, this involves *redemption* from the worship of other gods and from servitude to them. To use a biblical expression, men need to be redeemed from the prince of this age (John 12:31; 2 Cor. 4:4). Though God is sovereign, he is opposed in the heavenly places; and, though ultimately he will triumph, in this age the powers of wickedness challenge God's supremacy (Eph. 6:12; Luke 4:6). Where men accept this counter-claim to supremacy, they range themselves with these opposing forces (John 14:30).

Men also disown God's supremacy when they live their life on false foundations (Matt. 7:24; 1 Cor. 3:11). The word "world" is used in the New Testament again and again to denote life as organized apart from God (John 7:7; 14:17; Gal. 6:14). It is possible for man to base his life on the elements that constitute the "world's" foundation. The chief feature of these is that they offer to man an alternative to the life of faith (Gal. 4:3, 9; Col. 2:8, 20). Men must be redeemed from servitude to these.

And finally, men need to be redeemed from sin itself. By sin is meant not only the powers of evil outside man which assail the human soul (Luke 22:31; 1 Peter 5:8), but also the system from which sins derive and to which sinning contributes (John 8:34). Sinning organizes into a system, since sinful man naturally tends to create gods who will validate his life and his values. Idolatry is the very core of sin (John 9:39-41), and man needs to be redeemed from it (John 1:29; Rom. 6:23).

A. REDEEMED AND ADOPTED

Positively, therefore, *redemption* means that men are redeemed to faith in the Almighty and All-Sovereign God, and are accepted by him as sons (1 John 3:1; John 1:12). We have lost the sonship which was ours by the fact of creation; we become sons now through redemption (Luke 15:22; Rom. 8:15). Again, to use a biblical expression, *we are redeemed and adopted*.

God entered into history, challenged the prince of this age in his domain, and worsted him (Col. 2:15; John 16:11). The evil we now deal with is an evil that has been exposed and defeated. It is one thing to be asked to defeat evil; it is another thing to share in a victory already won (Col. 1:13-14).

Thus, when we speak of *redemption,* we remember (1) that it is God who did it; (2) that he paid the price of doing it; (3) that it has been done.

This is what is meant when the mission of Jesus is spoken of in terms of ransom (*lutron*) which is the root of the New Testament word for redemption (*lutrosis*) (Heb. 9:12; Luke 1:68; 2:38; Mark 10:45; 1 Tim. 2:6). For to be redeemed is simply to accept what God has done. And God has done something objective. *He has changed the context of man's earthly existence.* The sign of our acceptance of what God has done, whereby we ourselves are accepted as sons, is that now we say when we pray: "Our Father who art in heaven."

I believe in Jesus Christ—his Incarnation, redeeming work, and Lordship.

Therefore, I do not believe that sin is material (the Word became flesh), nor do I believe that there is salvation from sin by way of renunciation. But while sin is not material, it is original. It is there in all men, and it is there in all men from the beginning (Rom. 3:23). Men, therefore, cannot save themselves; they must be redeemed by God. And God has so worked for their redemption in Jesus Christ, in whom and through whom, whatever it costs, he seeks to love men back to himself who is their rightful Lord (Rom. 5:8; 2 Cor. 5:15). Hence it is that another of the essential elements of sin is the element of *adultery* —an act of infidelity against one's rightful Lord, and of ingratitude in spite of his abundant love.

Sin is an essential wrongness in man which only God's power and love can make right. It is not an imperfection that time will set right, or a disease that the psychotherapist can heal, or just ignorance which education will enlighten. Also, since sin is not material, there is not only a redemption from sin for the individual—there is a redemption of history and of nature too (Rom. 8:21). Where sin is thought of either as material or as eternal, one necessarily thinks of history as circular. Individuals are redeemed from the plane in which history moves, but history itself has no goal. It is a distinguishing mark of the Christian gospel that it speaks of redemption as being wrought both within and for history. Its conception of history is spiral, not circular. History is moving to an end. Of course, the Christian affirmation is not that history will reach its end by an immanent development, for history contains the cross, but that history will be redeemed since it contains the Incarnation. It will be redeemed by the power made manifest in the Resurrection of Christ. The day will dawn when sin itself shall be no more. Sin is not eternal; it will not be everlasting.

The essence of sin, then, lies in its relation to God. It is an offense against God's redeeming love. It is an act of ingratitude and disloyalty. It is *thuroham*. The Sinhalese word (*pau*) refers too exclusively to the result of sin on the sinner. It is a demeritorious act that entails a bad *kamma*. And in Tamil, too, the word *papam* is too exclusively a description of the condition of the sinner. Indeed, it is often used to describe a man who is in any pitiable condition, whether as a result of sinning or of poverty or of disease, so that what the *pavi* needs is pity. What the sinner needs, however, is not pity but forgiveness. Hence the necessity of the cross, for forgiveness is costly. It is costly to the forgiver, because it is a forgiveness of disloyalty, ingratitude, treachery. It is a specifically Christian doctrine that sinning puts not only man but also God into a pitiable predicament. Thus, to be forgiven is to have established the right relation to God's love, the relation of a wife's surrender to her husband. This is what faith is. It is an act of betrothal. Salvation from sin consists in an utter belonging to God (Rom. 7:4).

Negatively, this means *reconciliation* with God, whereas man is now alienated from him. In the first place, man's alienation from God consists and is due to man's declared independence. Man would rather be his own master (Gen. 3:5; John 12:25-26). If man is therefore to be reconciled to God, God himself must take the initiative and declare his love to hostile man (2 Cor. 5:19). Independence can be surrendered to love. It is doubt of God's love that lies at the root of this declaration of independence (Gen. 3:4-5).

Man's alienation from God is the result also of man's feeling of hopelessness, in that he thinks that he has forfeited forever the love of a holy God. Thus, reconciliation needs not only that God reveal a love which forgives, but also that he reveal a love which has forgiven (1 John 2:12). God forgives when I repent—that is Old Testament teaching; God has forgiven before I repent—that is New Testament teaching (Rom. 5:8).

Lastly, if reconciliation is to be complete, it needs not only a love that forgives, not only a love that has forgiven, but also a love whose forgiveness matters. Forgiving love, if it is to have reconciling power, must be able to forgive the sinner as well as his sin. To forgive the sinner means that the sinner's sin wounds the forgiver himself, for ultimately it is the sinner who matters to the forgiver. That is what happened to God in Jesus. He came to where sinners were and "was reckoned with the transgressors" (Luke 22:37; Isa. 53:12).

B. RECONCILED AND CONSECRATED

Positively, therefore, *reconciliation* means that we who have denied and wounded God's love are won back to and by that love to be to him again a people set apart, belonging to him alone (Titus 2:14). We are reconciled and consecrated (1 Peter 2:9). Once more, then, we see how God has acted on our behalf. He entered into history, met the sinner where he was, and though he was rejected by those who belonged to him (John 1:11), he would not let them go but died at their hands. It is one thing to be asked to love God; it is another thing to be asked to respond to God's love (1 John 4:10; Luke 7:47).

Thus, when we speak of *reconciliation* we remember (1) that it is God who did it; (2) that he paid the price of doing it; (3) that it has been done.

This is what Jesus means when he speaks of his mission in terms of calling sinners to repentance (Luke 5:32; 15:1-2), of seeking to induce in them *metanoia,* a change of mind. "Change" is also the root meaning of the New Testament word for reconciliation. It is this word which Paul uses to denote the fact of reconciliation between husband and wife (1 Cor. 7:11).

To be reconciled, therefore, is simply to respond to what God has done. And God has done something objective. *He has introduced into history a new power and possibility.* So that, as we accept the opportunity to live in true response to what God has done, we become his peculiar possession, bearing his name, as the wife bears the name of her husband. So we say when we pray: "Hallowed be thy name."

I believe in the Holy Spirit.

Therefore, I do not believe that sin consists either exclusively or primarily in breaking the rules of an ethical code, of a *dhamma* which is common to all men. It is specifically disobedience to God's will as he reveals it to me by his Spirit with respect to the choices and decisions of my life. Sin is *hamartia,* which means "to miss the mark," to live at random, not to fulfill the purpose of God for oneself. I am already the servant of sin, not concerned with knowing or doing God's specific will for me. In other words, sin is a religious rather than a moral category. Hence it is that another element of sin is the element of *blindness*. It is the result either of a culpable laziness of mind and of soul which refuses to seek or to accept more light, or of pride in one's present enlightenment. When the light that one has seen and accepted is treated as one's own enlightenment, it becomes an effective barrier against more light.

Thus, to speak of sin in a purely moral way is misleading. So is any comparison between the ethical attainments of the followers of the various religions. The crucial question is whether God wills every man to accept Jesus as Lord and Savior. Discipleship to Jesus is part of God's will for man. It is not simply an optional solution that God offers to men in their need. The religious quality of sin also means that there can be sin without there being a sense of guilt. Often the sense of guilt is absent because sin lies in some dark place in our lives where the light is not allowed to shine. It may be on the blind spot of our soul's vision. Also, the sense of guilt is blunted because we judge our actions in terms of our incapacity rather than in terms of the availability of God's power through his Spirit.

Again, then, we see that the essence of sin lies in its relation to God. The question is not whether one is good, but whether one is obedient. Sin is an offense against God's persisting purpose for men that they should become the sons of God. Sin is a falling short (Rom. 3:23). It is *thavaruthal*. Salvation from sin consists in concrete obedience to God (Rom. 14:8).

Negatively, this involves an act of *justification* by God even though God's law condemns. All men are under law and know that they are under law, whether it be the revealed law of the Jew or the natural law of the pagan (Rom. 1:19-20). But, whereas God intends his law to be for us a guide to our grateful response for all that he has done (Exod. 20:2; John 14:15), man, inasmuch as he is both unwilling to serve God as well as unable to get rid of God's commandments, changes God's law into a means of righteousness for himself (Luke 1:6; Phil. 3:6; Luke 18:21). The result is that he is condemned by the law (Rom. 7:7-25). It is not simply a question of being conscious of guilt and conscience-stricken; it is rather that one's status in God's world is the status of a condemned man.

But now that the love of God has become operative in the world as reconciling power, God confers on the condemned a new status. He is pronounced righteous (John 8:11; Rom. 8:1), and committed to live righteously, but henceforth in terms of forgiving love rather than in terms of demanding law (Rom. 3:21; 5:9; Matt. 5:20; Luke 16:16. Cf. Matt. 6:12; 1 John 1:7).

This is what Jesus means by his great invitation: "Come to me, all who labor . . . Take my yoke" (Matt. 11:28-29). It means a complete change of attitude before God's demands, the feeling of freedom in God's service. The yoke of the scribe is replaced by the yoke of the Christ. The law now is easy and its burden light. We are now working for him and not for a reward for ourselves, and there is exhilaration in the thought that we can trust him even with our mistakes (Phil. 3:8-14).

C. JUSTIFIED AND ENFRANCHISED

Positively, therefore, *justification* means a change of status, whereby, having received the King's amnesty, we are restored to free citizenship in the Kingdom (John 8:36; Eph. 2:17-19). We are justified and enfranchised. Here again we see how God has acted on our behalf. He has brought his Kingdom within the process of history, making possible a change in man's status itself. Man has no more to wait and prepare for the Kingdom; he can live by the fact that the Kingdom has already come (Rom. 5:20-21). It is one thing to be asked to build God's Kingdom; it is another thing to be asked to enter into it and to cause others to enter (Matt. 28:18-20; Acts 1; 3:6-8).

Thus when we speak of *justification,* too, we remember (1) that it is God who did it; (2) that he paid the price of doing it; (3) that it has been done.

This is what Jesus means when he speaks of his mission as the establishment of God's Kingdom into which the guilty will come (Matt. 21:31). They will accept the righteousness of God which pronounces righteous. Indeed the New Testament word *dikaiao* means to pronounce righteous and not to make righteous, so that to be justified is simply to accept what God has done. And God has done something objective. *He has altered the whole process of history*. He has brought in his Kingdom. So that we who are pardoned and set free, seek to live as we pray: "Thy kingdom come."

I believe in the holy Catholic Church, the communion of saints.

Therefore I do not believe that sin is a purely individual matter. It involves more than my individual relation to God. It involves my relation to the society of God's people. Here again the primary question is not whether I am good, but whether I am willing to accept the discipline, along with the privileges, of belonging to a larger whole. It is a specifically Christian doctrine that salvation from sin is social both in its method as well as in its result. I am saved through and for the Kingdom. Hence it is that another element of sin is being in a state of *lostness* (Matt. 18:11). The coin was lost from the necklace of coins where it belonged. The sheep was lost from the flock of sheep to which it belonged. The son was lost from the home to which he belonged. We are lost from membership in God's family to which we belong (Luke 15).

In other words, the church is the sphere in which the saved life has to be lived; it is not an option. The saved sinner belongs to it with all its faults, and his ultimate salvation depends on his acceptance of the discipline which is involved in his partaking of the church's privileges, in his sharing of its responsibilities and its mission, and in his bearing of its shame and weakness. Man is the responsible creature since he alone was made in God's image, that is, with a nature capable of responding to God and God's working.

Thus, once again we see how the essence of sin lies in its relation to God. It is an offense against God's activity in the world. It is a life of irresponsible aloneness. To sin is to be and become useless to God, to perish (John 3:16). It is *keduthal.* When a thing has perished, all that can be done with it is to burn it, to dispose of it. That is what Hell is, the place where rubbish is burnt, so that the Jews called Hell by the name of the valley in Jerusalem where they burnt rubbish—*Ge-Hinnom.* Salvation from sin consists in free usefulness to God (Rom. 12:1).

Negatively, this involves a *propitiation* for sin providing free forgiveness for the sinner. Man needs to be forgiven his willingness to disobey. Indeed, forgiveness for him means that his love for sin is radically dealt with, so that even though he may sin again he shall no more love sin. He who is born of God does not persist in sin (1 John 3:9; Rev. 1:5). Man needs to be forgiven also his actual acts of disobedience (Rom. 3:25), and most of all he needs to be forgiven the forfeiture of fellowship which that disobedience entails (1 John 1:6-7).

But how can this full forgiveness be effective when sinful man is both afraid and abased, and therefore unable to approach God and receive his forgiveness? To say that the knowledge of God's love as seen in Christ should give us boldness is only one part of the truth (Rom. 5:2); the other part of the truth is that it is only as we ourselves are in Christ that we feel able to stand in God's presence (Eph. 3:12). In other words, the moment of forgiveness is in Christ, God in Christ forgiving man in Christ (2 Cor. 5:17). It is this second truth of "man in Christ" in the moment of forgiveness which is set forth in the word "propitiation." Disobedient man comes into God's presence and pleads the merit of the obedient man (Rom. 5:19), the obedient man himself pleading for the disobedient one as his advocate (1 John 2:1-2; Heb. 4:15-16). Jesus is man's possibility and the guarantee of that possibility; so that man, in approaching God, is able to bring Jesus as his offering, his promise for the future (Heb. 7:22-25; 12:2).

D. FORGIVEN AND ENROLLED

Positively, then, *propitiation* signifies that man, who is unworthy to approach the Divine Presence, is able to approach it, for he comes covered by the "blood of Christ," i.e., by Christ's complete outpouring of his life in obedience to God which culminated in the cross (2 Cor. 10:5; Phil. 2:8; Rom. 5:13-18). It is so that man receives complete forgiveness; and, when forgiven, is also honored with the service of the same Christ in whom he was forgiven (2 Tim. 2:4). To be forgiven in Christ is to live in Christ forever. We are forgiven and enrolled. Thus we see again how God has acted on our behalf. He has provided us with the Captain of our salvation who will bring many sons unto glory (Heb. 2:10-11). It is one thing to be asked to work out our own salvation; it is another thing to have God working with us both to will and to work for his good pleasure (Phil. 2:12-13).

Thus, when we speak of *propitiation* also we remember (1) that it is God who did it; (2) that he paid the price of doing it; (3) that it has been done.

This is what Jesus means when he speaks of his mission as that of being man's true abiding place (John 15:5), for when man abides in him, man is in a propitious situation with respect to God. Thus in speaking about forgiveness through propitiation, we are speaking again of something that God has done. And he has done something objective. *He has provided a new ground for our being and living.* And now in his service we say when we pray: "Thy will be done."

I believe in the forgiveness of sins, the resurrection of the body, and the life everlasting.

I shall never do without the forgiveness of God, even if I strive to be perfect as he is perfect; and, at the last, it is by forgiveness that I shall be established. But established I shall be, for though sin is ever with me and in me, it has already received its death blow at the hands of Jesus Christ and its present power is but a carry-over, its last kick in its dying agony. The time will come when sin shall be no more, and our human life will be resurrected unto life eternal.

It is a true description of sin, then, to speak of it as our *predicament,* and to recognize that fundamentally sin, for us, consists in our transgression, *miruthal,* of the boundary of our own existence. We are creatures seeking equality with our Creator, so that to be saved means that we accept and abide in our creaturehood, praying humbly the creature's prayer: "Give and forgive, lead and deliver."

In summary, then, to be saved means that I am brought back to God because I am able to bring to God and offer back to him in glad acknowledgment what he has wrought for me. He redeemed and adopted me, reconciled and consecrated me, justified and enfranchised me, forgave and enrolled me; wherefore, I say when I pray: "For thine is the kingdom and the power and the glory for ever. Amen."

6.

The Christian Proclaims

In a sense this book is finished, and yet it is not quite finished until the Buddhist to whom this book is addressed has been helped, as it were, to overhear a conversation such as takes place between Christians when they speak together both about the task of evangelism as well as about the evangel. There are things which Christians say to each other in their own idiom which, if a Buddhist could listen to them, would give him just that additional insight into the meaning of the Christian faith which is so valuable. And essentially it is insight that is wanted, the sight within and from within, for the truest understanding of the Christian gospel comes only as one accepts and believes and enjoys.

A. THE GOOD NEWS OF GOD'S ACTION

How may we Christians make the preaching of the gospel meaningful? We talk of it as the good news of Christ, but hundreds of thousands of men and women deny that it is news at all. "News" is that which is significant for today and the needs of today. This definition is challenged by many in the West as applicable to the gospel, while many in the East ask whether the Christian gospel is even new.

What, for instance, does a missionary from the West come out to Ceylon to proclaim? If, in answer to a Buddhist, he says, "I have come to proclaim that God is and that God is love," he will get the inevitable reply, "Our scriptures also teach the way of love." And if the missionary answers, "Yes, but I have come to witness that that is the truth," the reply would simply be, "What is truth? Is it more than what is true for you?"

Whatever the missionary might reply to that, the answer which I would like to suggest is this: that we proclaim something that is truth for all, something which, because it is truth, is relevant for all time—the truth that God loved us in Jesus.

The gospel is not "God is love," but "God so loved." He so loved that he did something about it. He sent his Son, and that Son gave his life. The challenge of the gospel which we must face and which, having faced it, we in God's name must deliver to others is this: *"What have you done about what God has done for you? Have you given life for life, love for love, devotion for devotion?"*

Both in our New and Old Testaments, sin is described in a specifically religious way. A sinner is one who is out of fellowship, out of step, with God. He is in the wrong place. But we so often use the word "sin" purely in its moral sense, to denote just defects in character, that we miss the real significance of the biblical horror of sin. That God should take the initiative in visiting man, in doing something for man, fills the Bible with grateful wonder, and then to see men refuse to respond to God's action turns wonder into horror, the sense of gratitude into a sense of sin.

To sin is to refuse to meet God at the place where God has come to meet me. It is essentially an act of self-assertion. It is possible for man to be moral, good, and decent—and a sinner.

Again and again in India and Ceylon those who do evangelistic work are asked these questions: "What would you say to Mahatma Gandhi? Was he not morally a greater man than you?" —"Yes." "Had he not deeper spiritual insight than you?"—"Yes." What then would be your message to him? The same message. What have you done about what God has done for you in Jesus Christ? It is a question that all men must answer, including Mahatmaji, and in the face of that question, moral excellence and spiritual insight are an irrelevance.

Nicodemus was moral. Jesus told him to begin all over again, to be born anew. The elder brother who stayed with his father was moral. But he was at the same time prodigal from his father's love. The point simply is this—that the very morality we boast about may become the ground of our self-assertion, when it ought rather to be the fruit of our love for him who first loved us.

But, we must answer this question: Why, of all God's deeds, should it be necessary for us to make response to this deed of his in Jesus? Can we not pass it by? We can. And yet if we do, we shall never find God's answers to our own ultimate questions. At my deepest moments three questions constantly form in my mind—"Who am I? Why am I here? Where am I going?" And to these questions God makes answer by asking questions from his end. He asks them in Jesus about Jesus—"Who is he? Why is he here? Where is he going?" And it is only as I answer these questions that I find God's answers to my questions.

To refuse to answer God is to refuse God's answer to me.

B. THE DECISION WITHIN HISTORY

The thrust of this whole position lies here—that the doctrine of self-realization finds a new focus and orientation. Through the ages the quest has been to get beyond the finite to the infinite and beyond the temporal to the eternal.

But now, in that the Word has become flesh, the message and the offer of the gospel are that the self becomes real not by a flight from the finite and the temporal, but by choosing to take its stand at that point within the finite and temporal where finite and infinite, temporal and eternal, meet.

It is in facing us with the necessity of such a decision, a decision within the realm of history, that the gospel puts us on the spot with respect to our tendency to self-assertion. Without a real surrender of self, it is not possible to accept the claims of the historical Jesus.

Thus are men prevented in their decision from escaping into a realm of mere ideas and are called to choose within the realm of facts. They are no longer free to construct and worship myths, for he who demands worship has become history. They can no longer revel in the relativism of values, but are called to order by the objectivity of truth. Self-realization is to abide in Jesus.

But, in the presentation of the gospel and in its insistence on history, there is a real danger of pitching the gospel exclusively in the past. Jesus is a continuous fact. In seeking to say "God so loved," we must not forget the simple truth that "God so loves." He so loves that he is still doing something about it.

We say that the Incarnation is the turning point of history. What do we mean? The history of the world is and has always been the history of God's sovereignty, not that God is already supreme, but that his supremacy is always maintained; not that there is no strife with evil, but that God ultimately wins. But at the Incarnation there took rise, within this main current, a central stream which is the history of God's Incarnate Son, so that today, while all men stand in the main current of the history of God's sovereign rule, some stand also and more particularly in that stream which is the history of the body of Christ, the company of the redeemed, the community of the faithful. We are all his property, but to as many as receive him, he gives the authority to become sons (John 1:10-12).

The challenge of the gospel, therefore, is that men choose Jesus, not simply the so-called Jesus of history, but Jesus our contemporary both in his person and in his body—the church. It is a present fact to which we draw attention and for which we ask decision.

C. THE CHALLENGE OF THE KINGDOM

God's present activity of love, the fact that God so loves that he does something about it, may be presented in terms of three of the best-known statements of Jesus about the Kingdom.

The Kingdom of God is at hand. Turn around for God is behind you. How did God get there? He has been there all the time. He has been pursuing you, chasing you, hunting you down. Of how many of us is this not a true description: that our lives are characterized by flight, by panting breath and dilated eyes, fleeing from reality, fleeing from God. We may not turn around, but one thing we cannot do and that is get rid of him. He so loves.

The Kingdom of God is within your borders. It has invaded the territory of the soul, and it is laying siege. Surrender, for God is around you. He is pressing on all sides. Of how many of us is this not a true description: that our lives are cramped because God will not give us room. We need not surrender, but one thing we cannot do, and that is get rid of him. He so loves.

The Kingdom of God is upon you. It is here already. We may not repent; we may not surrender; but we still are subjects of the Kingdom. Because the Kingdom already is, we are already either citizens or rebels. We can choose to be either, but one thing we cannot do, and that is to contract out of God's rule. He so loves.

This gospel of God's present loving activity, in all its aspects, is the gospel of the Holy Spirit. Under the pressure of the tragedies that are all about us, we sometimes tend to make our hope of Christ's coming again to consummate his Kingdom a cloak to hide a secret fear that as far as today is concerned God is more or less absent and the devil is in charge. Even talk of obedience to God's secondary orders of creation, as God's will for us in this in-between time can be dangerous. We dare not and cannot forget that God calls us even now to give him the fruits of his vineyard of which we are already his husbandmen.

The church must be a part of the gospel. That the church exists must be good news for the world. And it is the church's task in itself to be a fact which disturbs the world calling it to repentance, which oppresses the world calling it to surrender, and which reminds the world of God's rule calling it to obedient acceptance.

The significance of this is that the problem of salvation is thrown into full relief disclosing the fact that redemption is not to be in any sense redemption from life and its interests, but redemption of life itself from sin and the power of Satan. Life itself is good and is charged with Divine purpose and is undergirded with Divine active love.

But no talk of the Christian community as part of the gospel should lead us to make people believe that the Kingdom of God stands or falls with us, and still less that we can build the Kingdom. We cannot build the Kingdom because it is more than a temporal order. When it is established, death and sin shall be no more, and there will be not only a new earth but also a new heaven. Neither will the Kingdom stand or fall with us for, though every man may prove faithless, yet God remains and will remain true.

But is not the Kingdom to be also a present reality? Is not God's rule to be made operative now in human affairs? Yes, but while we are called upon to lead men to accept God's reign as a personal commitment and to work for the establishment of the values of the Kingdom in human affairs, yet to us is not given either the power or the authority to guarantee a world where either those who build their houses upon sand or those who build their houses upon rock will be safe from storm and flood (Matt. 7:24-27). Indeed, that we believe and proclaim that the Kingdom will finally come in power and in glory is based not so much on what we can see God doing now in and through his children as on what God is. He loved. He loves. He will love unto the end.

It is this gospel which it is our task to proclaim. Our task is to proclaim it so that men of every background can understand it. It is not our task, however, to make it either acceptable or reasonable. The Jews found the gospel unacceptable; to them it was a stumbling block. The Greeks found the gospel unreasonable; to them it was foolishness. But Paul was concerned only with the task of making the gospel understandable. When we try to make the gospel acceptable or reasonable we inevitably tend to change its content. Let the group to whom we have to proclaim the gospel determine how we are to proclaim it, but let it not affect what we are to proclaim. There is timeliness today in Paul's resolution to preach Christ in foolishness of words.

D. THE NECESSITY OF CONVERSION

One insistent question remains to be faced with regard to the whole program of evangelism, and that is the place and value of the spread of Christian ideas, of making so-called unconscious Christians. A useful approach to this question is to consider the difference that there is between three types of conversion:

First of all, there is conversion to the Christian community: *proselytization.* This is on the whole what has happened in mass-movement areas in India or Indonesia. The choice these masses have made is to go from one community in which they feel they have no place and no hope to the Christian community. That these proselytes are later on through education, nurture, and discipline converted to Jesus is true, but it is later. Still, this process is valid because not only is the choice of the Christian community as a social and spiritual home a choice within the meaning of the gospel, but also because the condemnation of proselytization lies in treating it as sufficient and so an end in itself.

The danger, however, is that those engaged in this work should tend to raise secondary issues in the minds of those among whom they work, and also tend in such a way to point to secondary results of joining the Christian community so as to make these results have a bribe-appeal.

The second type is conversion to Christian ideas and ideals: *Christianization*. But while this is an inevitable result of Christian living and teaching, it is not the satisfying objective of Christian work.

Our task is so to work and pray that men may be converted to Jesus: *evangelism*. We must live as helpful lives as possible, for we already are Christians. We must teach Christian ideas and ideals and live them, for we already are Christians. But we must be satisfied with ourselves only when we have helped men and women to enter into a personal relationship with God in Jesus. Jesus cured ten lepers for they all needed healing. He was satisfied that his work was done only with the leper who came back and gave God thanks.

But can we convert? No, and we are not asked to. Our task is to lift Christ up in word and in life, and it is his promise that he will draw men to himself. We preach not a dead Jesus as an example to be imitated, but a risen Christ as a person to be followed. No one who does not take the resurrection of Jesus seriously can be an evangelist.

What do we hope to see as a result of this work? We hope to see in each place an indigenous church and an indigenous Christianity. The gospel is the seed which one plants in the different soils of different peoples. The plant that grows up is Christianity. It bears marks both of the soil and of the seed. Each place must grow its own plant. The old days when missionaries took potted-plants is over. It is only the gospel which it is important to bring.

There are problems, of course. We must see that the plant does not bear more marks of the soil than of the seed, a problem which exists in the West as acutely as it exists in the East. And then there is the still greater danger of attempting not to grow a plant from the gospel-seed at all, but to use the gospel as a fertilizer to give added qualities to the natural plant already flourishing in the country's soil. This is what the program of Christianization amounts to when treated as a complete objective.

The church already exists in almost every country, the result of the labor of love of many generations of missionaries, the fruit of the living of countless thousands of its own people. May this church in every place, through danger and difficulty, trial and temptation, in wrestling of thought and witness of life, fulfill its place in the total Christian testimony to the variegated pattern of God's working.

Glossary

ahimsa—non-violence, non-infliction of pain
amata—undying, immortal
anatta—soul-less-ness, absence of self
anicca—impermanence, transistoriness
araha—worth
arahat—worthy one
atta—soul, self
avijja—ignorance
Buddha—the Enlightened One
buddhi—intelligence, knowledge
dana—generosity, almsgiving
dhamma—law, doctrine, right
doha—disloyalty, hatred *dm*
dukkha—sorrow, care
iddhi—psychic power
jhana—meditation, psychic trance
kamma—result of action, chain of causation
karuna—compassion, mercy
keduthal—to perish
kusala—merit, skill, good
metta—friendliness, affection
miruthal—to trangress
mudita—gentleness
nana—wisdom
nibbana—emancipation, state of release
nicca—eternal, permanent, timeless
panna—wisdom, vision
pansil—the five precepts
papa—sin
parami—virtue, perfection
pattidana—transference of merit
pavam—sin
samadhi—poise, rest
sangha—the community of monks
sansara—the cycle of existence
sarana—refuge, protection
sila—virtue, holiness, goodness
skandha (or *kandha*)—aggregate-*the sense*
tanha—desire, craving, thirst
tapo—penance, austerity
thavaruthal—to fall short
thuroham—ingratitude, disloyalty
upekkha—equanimity
virodham—opposition, rebellion